GW01003335

The Indian Ocean –
Goa, Sri Lanka
& The Maldives

REG BUTLER

In Association with

THOMSON HOLIDAYS

SETTLE PRESS

Text © 1994 Reg Butler
3rd Edition 1997

First published by Settle Press
10 Boyne Terrace Mews
London W11 3LR

ISBN (Paperback) 1 872876 60 9

Printed by Villiers Publications
19 Sylvan Avenue
London N3 2LE
Maps by Mary Butler

Foreword

As Britain's leading holiday company operating to Goa and other beach destinations of the Indian Ocean, Thomson are happy to be associated with Reg Butler's latest guide-book to the region.

The author has travelled annually for around two dozen years throughout India and other areas, and is well qualified to write about the history, culture and cuisine of these fascinating lands.

Whichever destination you have chosen for your holiday, we feel this pocket book can act as a quick reference guide to the great sightseeing potential beyond the beaches. In writing the book, the author has also worked closely with our own locally-based staff and agents who have year-round contact with holidaymakers' travel interests.

Prices are always a problem during a time of variable inflation and exchange rates. Inevitably there will be some local changes since this edition was printed. However, the prices mentioned should still give a reasonable indication of the average level of expenses to expect.

THOMSON HOLIDAYS

Contents

Chapter One

Introduction

1.1 Indian Ocean highlights

The third largest ocean after the Pacific and Atlantic, the Indian Ocean covers about one-fifth of the world's water surface.

It is eight times the size of USA, stretching from the Red Sea and Persian Gulf to the borders of Indonesia; along the entire east coast of Africa to the longitude of the Cape of Good Hope; and past the west coast of Australia to Antarctica.

In the tropical zones the water temperature stays generally above an idyllic 80^0 F. This constant temperature is perfect for the off-shore growth of coral reefs. In turn, the coral attracts shoals of variegated tropical fish, while providing sheltered lagoons between the reef and the sandy shorelines.

All these conditions are ideal for modern holiday-makers who dream of warm sunshine, uncrowded beaches, choice of watersports – including snorkelling among the fish – and a hotel set amid rustling palm trees.

In Goa and Sri Lanka, the long beaches are far removed from industry and big cities. Visitors can enjoy the crystal-clear waters, while having rich sightseeing within easy reach. It's certainly worth tearing oneself away from the golden sands, to savour the cultures of India and old-time Ceylon.

Most of the widely scattered tropical islands of the Indian Ocean were virtually uninhabited until 500 years ago – mainly due to their remote locations, far removed from historic trading routes. Only a few Arab sailors, and then the Portuguese and the Dutch, knew first-hand of the existence of the Maldive Islands.

In contrast to medieval times, when trading dhows hugged the shorelines of Africa and Asia, the Indian Ocean today is a major transportation highway for oil tankers from the Middle East to Southeast Asia, the Pacific and the Americas. Factory ships exploit the ocean mainly for shrimp and tuna.

Otherwise the seas remain as empty as ever. It's the age of air transport which has opened these tropical paradise destinations to holidaymakers and honeymooners in search of somewhere 'different'.

One can explore and enjoy the Robinson Crusoe scenery in a setting of total comfort.

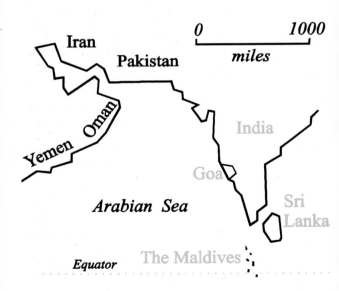

Chapter Two

Planning to go

2.1 Which season?

Whichever month you choose for Indian Ocean destinations, there'll be guaranteed warm sun. The seasons are mainly determined by the monsoon wind system. North of the equator, northeast winds blow from October until April; from May until October, the winds come from south and west.

Goa has three seasons: winter, summer and wet monsoon. The best holiday months are November to March, bone dry and comfortably warm. April until mid-June becomes extremely hot. Then the monsoon takes over with a total 88" of rain until it dries up in October.

Other parts of India can vary greatly in total rainfall and also in the seasonal pattern. In Madras, for instance, the light rains of the South West Monsoon occur between June and September, followed by the heavier rains of October and November from the North East Monsoon.

The northern cities of Delhi, Agra and Jaipur can be cool enough for wearing a sweater even in daytime during the winter months of December to February, followed by grilling heat in May and June. The rains are concentrated into July-September.

In Sri Lanka the pattern is somewhat different, with rains peaking in April-June and in October-November. Year-round there is little difference in the average maximum temperatures, around 85°.

In the Maldives, the rainy season is from May to November, with the heaviest rainfalls in June and July, when there's also a small dip in temperatures.

9

2.2 The weather to expect:

Max — Average maximum temperatures — °F.   Rain — Monthly rainfall in inches.

	Jan	Feb	Mar	Apr	May	Jun	Jul	Aug	Sep	Oct	Nov	Dec	Annual rainfall
GOA													
Max	89	90	90	91	91	87	84	84	85	88	91	91	
Rain	0.1	0.0	0.2	0.4	0.7	22.8	35.1	13.4	10.9	4.8	0.8	1.5	90.7"
DELHI													
Max	70	75	86	97	106	104	95	93	93	95	84	73	
Rain	1.0	0.9	0.7	0.3	0.3	2.6	8.3	6.8	5.9	1.2	0.0	0.2	28.2"
MADRAS													
Max	84	88	91	95	100	99	95	95	93	90	84	82	
Rain	0.9	0.3	0.6	1.0	2.0	2.1	3.3	4.9	4.6	10.5	12.2	5.5	47.9"
COCHIN													
Max	88	88	88	88	88	84	82	82	82	84	86	86	
Rain	0.3	1.3	2.0	5.5	14.3	29.8	22.5	15.2	9.2	13.1	7.2	1.5	121.9"
SRI LANKA													
Max	86	87	88	88	87	85	85	85	85	85	85	85	
Rain	3.5	2.5	6.0	9.0	14.5	9.0	5.5	4.5	6.5	13.5	12.5	6.0	93.0"
MALDIVES													
Max	87	86	87	91	93	93	87	84	86	87	87	86	
Rain	1.8	1.3	1.2	2.3	7.4	12.0	9.3	8.0	6.5	7.2	6.5	3.4	66.9"

2.3 Visa regulations

UK, EC, Commonwealth or US citizens do not need visas for Sri Lanka, or the Maldives. But everyone must have a six-month visa for India before travelling. Costing £26, this is obtainable from High Commission of India, India House, Aldwych, London WC2B 4NA. Tel: 0171-836-8484.

Visas can also be obtained from the India Consulate, 20 Augusta Street, Hockley, Birmingham B18 6JL. Tel: 0121-212-2782.

2.4 What to pack and what to wear

Pack light cotton dresses of the drip-dry wash-and-wear variety, and a lightweight suit for up-market evening dining. A wide brimmed beach hat and sun glasses are recommended, and comfortable shoes or sandals. Bring plastic shoes as protection from sharp coral if you're keen on snorkelling or underwater sports. Visitors should be suitably clad when entering temples and shrines.

Hotels provide basic equipment for the usual holiday sports. But dedicated tennis players, for instance, should bring their favourite tennis gear.

2.5 Health care

There is no *obligation* to produce vaccination certificates when arriving direct from Europe or North America. But some jabs are recommended, and vaccination records should be checked.

Ask your own doctor's advice at least six weeks before departure. Some medical people lean heavily towards ultra-caution, and recommend the full works. Others suggest that some jabs are not essential if you are taking normal care of yourself, and not visiting any outlandish areas.

For further health advice contact the Hospital for Tropical Diseases Healthline on 0839 337 722. Code number is 55. A phone charge is made of 36p a minute in off-peak hours; otherwise 49p a minute.

Mosquitoes

Quite apart from the dreaded female *anopheles* mosquitoes who spread malaria, have your defences ready against all the other varieties of biting insects. Mosquitoes and sand flies bite especially at dusk when hungry for supper. They are very partial to holidaymakers. Be frugal with perfumes and after-shaves, as these seem to attract them. Insect repellents are sold at chemists and in hotel-resort shops.

An excellent mosquito deterrent is (believe-it-or-not) Avon's 'Skin-so-soft' bath oil spray. It's highly effective. Even sand flies will keep their distance.

Chapter Three

Golden sands of Goa

3.1 History and beaches

250 miles south of Bombay, as the charter aircraft flies down the west coast of India, long stretches of golden beach are backed by lush green countryside.

Occupied by the Portuguese in 1510, the city of Old Goa became the capital of all Portuguese territories in India, and later the administration and religious centre for Portugal's entire empire in the East. The broad estuaries and natural harbours made Goa an ideal base.

For a hundred years the Portuguese kept their trading monopoly in India until the Dutch and then the English established settlements in other areas of the sub-continent. Bypassed for the next few centuries, Goa slumbered in a tranquil backwater until Portugal's 450 years of colonial rule ended in 1961.

The 65 miles of Goan coastline were 'discovered' by the hippies of the 1960's. Attracted by the golden beaches of superb quality, the drop-outs of 30 years ago flocked to this idyllic winter paradise where fish, rice and alcohol were cheap, and a palm-thatched hut could be rented for peanuts.

Following the hippy pioneers, developers built resort hotels that catered for much wealthier visitors. Finally the charter flights arrived, to reinstate Goa as an international gateway into the Indian sub-continent.

The way is now open for holiday visitors to combine the pleasures of a tropical beach with the chance of seeing some of the great sightseeing highlights of India.

N

MAHARASHTRA

Chapora Fort

Vagator
Anjuna
Baga
Calangute
Candolim
Aguada Fort

Beaches

Mapusa

Old Goa

PANAJI

Aguada Bay
Dona Paula
Mormugao

Miramar
Siridao

Shri Manguesh Temple

Khandepar
Ponda

Vasco da
Gama
Bogmalo

Velsao
Cansaulim
Majorda

Shri
Shantadurga
Temple

Colva
Benaulim

Varca

Margao

Resort Beaches

Arabian
Sea

Cavelossim
Mabor
Betul

COASTAL GOA

0   5   10
miles

In contrast to the famous tourist cities and teeming populations elsewhere in India, the largest town and capital of Goa is Panaji (also known as Panjim) with 60,000 people. Most of the remaining 1.2 million inhabitants live in villages. Many of their houses are built of red laterite stone or brick, with several rooms and a verandah. It could be southern Portugal, transplanted among the coconut groves and banyan trees.

Wherever you stay at the developing beach resorts, this life of rural India is only a short walk away. A drive through the evergreen countryside is beautiful everywhere.

All along the coast is a lush belt of coconut groves, with tranquil villages in the shade. Bullock carts take produce to market, while cattle wander in leisured style across the road, heedless of scooters.

The inland hills are a beautiful feature of Goa. Winding country roads pass terraced fields and a myriad fruit trees. Here is the land of cashew nuts, Goa's largest export crop.

A favourite tourist excursion is to a model fruit and spice farm, to watch the harvesting of coconuts, and inspect the plants and trees which produce the ingredients of India's famous curries and chutneys. Most visitors go home with low-cost packets of spices and cashew nuts.

Tropical fruits are part of the holiday. Stubby little bananas have a delicious sweet flavour, far tastier than Britain's imported bananas which are picked green for transport, and ripened artificially. Likewise the local pineapples are sweet and juicy, and served in fat slices.

The best eating in Goa is seafood, cooked in a variety of styles. Along the beaches, shack restaurants serve lobster, tiger prawns, squid, oysters, mussels, crabs, shark mullet, pomfret, grouper and mackerel at less than one-third the cost in hotels and more formal restaurants. However, be cautious! Snack restaurants are not controlled for health and safety. Hygienic standards can be dubious, and customers are taking a chance on falling ill.

There's no such thing as a crowded beach. The sands are powder-fine, often several hundred yards deep from the shoreline to the palm trees. Colva Beach is the longest on India's west coast.

Very little is left of the hippy scene of 30 years ago, though a few veterans base themselves at Anjuna Beach, where an ultra-simple room costs only £2 or £3 a night.

The beach resorts are low profile. As a later starter in holiday business, the Goan authorities want to avoid the shoe-box architecture of Mediterranean resorts. Instead, holiday bungalows and villas are set amid gardens and palm trees, with social life revolving around the pool.

Service standards are average, but friendly. Goans have long been recruited as staff aboard the world's great cruise liners. Experienced stewards, bar-tenders and musicians have come ashore and by example are training the younger generation.

Nobody goes to Goa for the nightlife, but beach barbecues and folk entertainment add pleasure to the evenings. Goan music and dancing is a rich cultural mixture of Hindu and Portuguese.

The favourite musical instrument is the guitar. Popular tunes are sung either in Portuguese or in the Goan mother tongue of Konkani. Many dances and costumes have come direct from Portugal.

The Portuguese heritage is seen especially in the religion. At Christmas there are serenades of guitars, mandolins and violins, with the singing of popular carols and the Portuguese love songs called fados. Nearly 40% of the population are Catholics.

Certainly Goa has a character quite distinct from the rest of India. Skirts far outnumber saris and people display an easy going tropical indulgence and civility which you will find hard to beat. Markets are lively colourful affairs and siesta is observed during the hot afternoons.

Although beaches are the focus of a Goan holiday, there is good sightseeing potential within an easy drive. The great churches of Old Goa are World Heritage Monuments and the scene of Catholic pilgrimage. Only a short distance away are equally interesting Hindu temples which likewise are pilgrim sites. Above all, there is constant pleasure from that beautiful green countryside.

3.2 Arrival & orientation

Coming in from the north, the aircraft offers a good view of Goa's north coast beaches. First you see the estuary of the River Mandovi – the boundary between the districts of North and South Goa – immediately followed by the much broader Mormugao Bay, which is fed by the River Zuari. Then you see the major cargo terminal of Mormugao itself, which handles Goa's iron ore exports.

The aircraft circles south of Vasco da Gama, which takes its name from the Portuguese explorer; and then flies over Bogmalo Beach for the landing.

Goa's airport has a vintage Portuguese appearance. A poster may still proclaim 1991 as the Year of Indian Tourism, and a welcoming sign in mid-March can wish everyone a Merry Christmas and Happy New Year.

Standing half an hour for immigration rituals, visitors soon get the message that the pace of life is rather more sedate than elsewhere.

Customs clearance is simple. You are expected to declare the more costly electronic and photographic items, and must pay duty if they are not re-exported when you depart. A faded notice says that five rolls of camera film are the limit for what may be brought in. But there are no searching questions on this point.

Outside the terminal, the travel agency reps and tour buses await. It's a 45-minute journey to Panaji – an essential staging-point for people staying at any of the north beaches. For the south beaches, transfer time is a maximum of 75 minutes. Wherever you're staying, the gorgeous scenery en route is already part of the holiday experience.

3.3 At your service

Money: Subject to fluctuation, the exchange rate of the Indian rupee is around 50 Rs to the pound, or 33 Rs to the US dollar. Currency and travellers cheques are readily exchanged at about the same rate in banks or hotels.

Some banks can give cash against Visa or Access/Mastercard. Passports are required for exchange transactions. Ensure that you are given a receipt, which is required for converting back any remaining rupees on departure.

Transport: Goa now has a reasonable highway system, though local driving techniques may seem hair-raising. Goan road-users often combine Latin panache with a Hindu fatalism that gives them sublime confidence that there'll be nothing coming the other way if they overtake on a bend.

A high proportion of the local male population rides around on scooters and motor-bikes, and even a minority of the women and girls, but hardly anyone wears a helmet.

Along tarred roads there is room for about 1½ vehicles, with dirt shoulders on either side. Whoever is chicken can make a last-second swerve into the dust. Wobbling bicycles and aimless animals are an additional hazard.

The message is that motor-bike or car hire is not recommended. However, if you are determined on vehicle rental, come equipped with an International Driving Licence, as the regular licence is not recognised in India. If stopped by a policeman, an on-the-spot fine is levied on anyone without a proper International Licence.

If caught, haggle! The fine can come tumbling down if you protest that you are carrying very little cash. Having negotiated your fine, it's unlikely that any receipt will be given. It all helps policemen to top up their low salaries.

Travelling by local bus is another non-tempting experience. Buses are tightly packed, run to erratic timetables and are liable to delays and breakdowns. However, they are extremely cheap.

There are also more comfortable long-distance inter-State services that are described as Luxury or Air-Conditioned. For the distances involved they are very economical. To Bombay, for instance, the 16-hour 370-mile journey costs under £5.

For local trips, taxis are the answer; or car-rental with driver, which is virtually the same thing.

The best bet in Goa are the white tourist vehicles that stand outside hotels. At many cab-ranks, a display board states the cost to sundry destinations. It's usual to arrange a set fee for a return journey, plus 10 to 20 rupees per hour waiting time. In fact the return journey normally costs little more than single.

Most of the drivers are helpful and courteous, and are familiar with the highlights of tourism. But they are not trained guides. They will cheerfully wait for hours while you sun-bathe on a beach or enjoy a leisurely lunch. But you cannot expect any in-depth explanation of local customs.

If you want an informed commentary and a well-planned itinerary, take the travel-agency sightseeing tours by coach or minibus. The experience of India is not just a question of admiring the scenery and sampling the different beaches. It also comes from getting a deeper understanding of the cultural background, with a well-educated guide to answer questions and explain the Goan lifestyle. Tour programmes often include a traditional Goan lunch and even feature some folklore entertainment.

City taxis

In cities like Panaji – and in the other cities of India – there are regular yellow-top taxis (usually vintage Indian-made Ambassador cars that are old-time Morris Oxford design). If their meter still works, make sure it is turned on.

Owing to inflation, fares do not always conform to readings on the meter. To avoid confusion, ask to see the latest fare chart, and pay accordingly.

There are also auto rickshaws, which are fun and very cheap for short rides. Even cheaper for the ultra-brave are motor-cycle 'taxis' for one passenger only, riding pillion. Not recommended.

For railway buffs, Goa was formerly served only by one line from Bombay to Margao and Vasco da Gama – a 24-hour ordeal.

However, a new rail link called Konkan Railway started operating in 1995, taking only 8 hours for the same journey. By air, Bombay is 60 minutes away; Delhi 2½ hours.

3.4 Cultural background

Goa offers a unique cultural mixture of India and Portugal, Hindu and Catholic. Religions co-exist amicably in Goa, which has never had inter-communal violence.

Religious festivals come with great frequency, and are usually celebrated by all the communities. Hindus keep Christmas and enjoy Carnival; Catholics take time off for Shigmo, the Hindu springtime counterpart of Carnival. It's worth making local enquiry about any festivities scheduled during your stay, to enjoy one of these colourful events.

Around 38% of the population are devout Catholics. Goan women wear white or black lace mantillas to Mass, while the Catholic religion is interwoven with the caste system (at least so far as marriage eligibility is concerned). Catholic processions are lively with fire-crackers in the church precincts.

The Catholic creed was established by the Franciscans who arrived in 1517. But the greatest religious fervour came from the Jesuits in mid-16th century, under the inspired leadership of St Francis Xavier who spread his missionary work throughout Asia. Besides their missionary work, the Jesuits also opened schools, founded a hospital and established a printing press.

Possibly that explains the higher literacy level of the Goan people, who are very successful in computer industries, politics, medicine and other professions. Many Goans work in the Gulf, earning good money which they send back home – often returning to start their own successful businesses, based on experience acquired abroad.

After 450 years of Portuguese influence, Goans talk with Latin gesticulations, have a cheerful and optimistic character, and enjoy an afternoon siesta. The parish schools conducted classes in singing, piano and violin playing, which is reflected today in Goan musical skills.

Many folk-tunes come direct from Portugal. In music, dance and costume there is a marriage of cultures, which also appears in the local cuisine.

3.5 Beach-hopping in south Goa

Goa's tourist industry is built on sand, though the physical accommodation is set well back from the shoreline (no building within 200 metres of the High Tide Line), with strict height restrictions within a 500-metre zone. Foreshore developments have been rigidly controlled in this way since 1991, to preserve the natural look that is one of Goa's greatest shoreline assets.

Only two other States in India regulate tourism in this environmentally friendly way. There is no threat that Goa will become a Spanish-style Costa lined with high-rise concrete.

Wherever you're staying, it's easy to go beach-hopping by scooter or taxi. Organised tours combine a selection of beaches with other sightseeing. Roads go north-south, parallel to the coastline through miles of lush coconut plantations. Minor side-roads turn down to the beaches that are strung like a golden necklace along the entire coast.

Scattered amid the palm groves are the land-owners' spacious bungalows, well shaded and traditional in style except for satellite dishes. Notice the stone benches on every verandah, where family and friends exchange gossip.

Colva Beach is the second longest in India, outstripped only by Marina Beach at Madras on the east coast. Four miles from Margao, Colva has adequate shopping, refreshment and changing facilities for day-trip visitors. Everyone can have an acre of space, along a beach that's two hundred yards wide from the ocean to the shoreline palm trees. The sea is warm as new milk.

Facing the village centre of Colva, fishing boats are anchored just offshore, and outriggers are hauled up on the beach. Fishermen spread out their catch to dry in the wind. If you're fond of seafood, the aroma is heavenly.

Otherwise you can choose from literally miles of golden sand – south to the more secluded beaches of **Benaulim**, **Cavelossim** and **Mabor**; or north towards **Betalbatim** and **Majorda**. They all offer a

scattered range of accommodation from resort hotels
to tourist bungalows. A few beach bars and seafood
restaurants cater to western tastes. Evening time is
great for a stroll, especially with a refreshing sea
breeze to help you cool down from the midday
heat.

Going north past Majorda, there's another long
stretch of beaches – **Cansaulim** and **Velsao** – and
thence round to **Bogmalo**, the closest to the airport,
only three miles away. Part of that beach is well
manicured for guests of a dominant 7-storey hotel –
one of the few beachfront properties, built before
the stricter building regulations were applied.

Nestling between the Arabian Sea and the Zuari
River, **Vasco da Gama** is Goa's most cosmopolitan
town. Known locally just as Vasco, it is well laid
out in comparison to other Goan towns. It is equi-
distant from Dabolim airport and the port of Mormugao which is one of India's major natural harbours, handling very large exports of iron ore.

Vasco is a showcase for wood carvings and
handicrafts, handled by several shops near the northern end of Swatantra Path. However, there's not
much else to interest keen shoppers. A mile from
Vasco is **Baina Beach**, half of which is reasonable,
while the other half is rather seedy due to its prox-
imity to a notorious red light area that serves Mormugao.

Across the wide Mormugao Bay a number of
delightful small coves are spaced along the foreshore of the Zuari estuary. Typical of several pleasant holiday beaches is **Dona Paula**, which offers
facilities for water scootering. A dozen outrigger
fishing boats are pulled up on the sands. Further
round the bay, pleasure boats and foreshores are
dedicated to holiday use. All these beaches are
within very easy reach of Panaji.

Around the headland into Aguada Bay, **Miramar
Beach** stretches along a river promenade into Panaji
itself. It's a good beach, with wide, golden sand.
Here is the setting for a Food and Cultural Festival
held annually in the third week of November, and
also for Carnival in mid-February. In late March
the Shigmo festival heralds the coming of Spring.

3.6 Beach-hopping in north Goa

The Mandovi River marks the boundary between south and north Goa, with the bridges at Panaji providing the principal highway link.

Dominating the northern tip of the estuary is Fort Aguada, which looks out to sea and across to Miramar Beach and Panaji. The huge Portuguese fortress, built square and formidable, is now used as a prison.

Aguada means 'watering place'. In Aguada Bay below the Fort, Portuguese ships traditionally took on their supplies of fresh water for the long voyage home. Today, the watering place is infinitely peaceful, with just a few water buffaloes and some fishing vessels around the landing-stage.

Along the road to the lighthouse beside the prison-fortress, one gets a fine panorama of the ruler-straight beach that stretches north. It goes from Fort Aguada Beach Resort through **Sinquerim Beach** and **Candolim Beach** to **Calangute** and thence to the estuary of the next major river at **Vagator**. The beaches are deep soft sand all the way.

Parallel to the coast, the highway is being ribbon developed with spacious houses in large gardens. Some are used as guest houses. A number of Tibetan and Kashmiri establishments display their handicrafts.

Blocks of the red laterite stone, quarried from local hillsides, are piled ready at building sites. There are even landscape developers at work among the new shop complexes, studios and apartments.

You can see all the growth stages of this new industry of catering for visitors.

First a shack is established on a suitable patch of land. With a roof of thatch or corrugated iron, and matting supported by poles for the walls, a man is in business: a refreshment stand, fast Indian food, a bar, a grocery kiosk or a souvenir stall.

Later the walls are made more permanent with laterite building blocks. Then comes painting and decorating, and tiling of the roof, until it all looks quite pristine in contrast to the original shack.

Calangute is the main focus of all this activity, and rates as Goa's most developed beach resort, with easy access to Mapusa and Panaji. This is one of the original hippy beaches, but it's now well served with a full range of hotels, guest houses, restaurants and tourist shops. There are rooms to let, cycles for hire and tourist taxis.

However, the village character is still preserved around Calangute Market, where farmers park their bullock carts in the shade of coconut palms. Just opposite the market is a brightly-coloured Hindu temple.

Baga Beach lies two miles north: a former fishing village, somewhat quieter than Calangute. The two resorts are virtually merging into one, as space is filled with more hotel developments.

The road between Calangute and Anjuna offers gorgeous scenery with green hillsides, fields, coconut palms and plentiful birdlife. White and black goats browse across the harvested fields like gleaners at work.

Anjuna Beach was known as the hippies' heaven, but relatively few aging survivors remain, renting a room or a house for the winter. The beach is set in a series of little coves overlooked by purple cliffs. On Wednesdays a general flea market is held, where people from miles around bring their handicraft products. The few designer hippies are greatly outnumbered by the Kashmiris and the Tibetans.

Vagator and **Small Vagator** are within walking distance of Anjuna. Vagator beach is often used as a locale for film shooting. Overlooking the beach is Chapora Fort, on the crest of a headland that commands entry into Chapora River.

Both at Anjuna and Vagator are faded notices that remind today's visitors of the area's former notoriety in the Indian press. The wording is still readable: "Nudism is Prohibited"; or "Don't dabble in drugs. It is a social crime, punishable with ten to thirty years imprisonment."

A beachside shack restaurant offers very basic furnished rooms at £3 a night, with a notice at the entrance: "Beware of touts and drug dabblers."

24

3.7 Shopping

Market centres
Regular shop hours are Mon-Fri 9-13 and 16-20
hrs, while street markets are more flexible. Friday
is the most popular shopping day for local people.
Panaji is the principal shopping centre, but the
colourful traditional markets at Margao and Mapusa
are much more fun, with something different again
at Anjuna Beach.

Margao, twenty miles from Panaji, is the congested
market centre and administrative capital for south
Goa. With major bus and rail terminals, it's the
thriving hub of trading and business. The city
boasts fine parks and gardens, and imposing Portu-
guese-built mansions and contemporary buildings.

There are four market places in central Margao:
municipal market, fish market, vegetable market
and new market. The new market is simply an old
market which moved closer into town. The vegetable market is also known as Modki Bazaar, where
pots and earthenware are sold.

An indoor market is located near the garden
square. It's worth visiting for the interesting sights
and smells, thanks to a good range of spices, nuts
and leather sandals. Regular shops sell handicrafts,
clothes and giftware. Photo stores can develop and
print your films at around 200 Rs for 24 prints.

Mapusa is north Goa's principal crossroads and
market centre with daily activity that peaks on Friday into a big tourist attraction. It's a good place to
buy local crafts and souvenirs, and enjoy the hustle
and bustle. Gold and silver jewellery is sold here;
and the drums called tabla; spices; readymade gar-
ments; nuts; liquors.

Peasant farmers display their produce while sit-
ting, squatting or lying on the ground. Fruit is neat-
ly arranged in pyramids. There are grapes on sale,
garlands and garlic. Overall is a tantalising medley
of different smells: some good, some bad. Fresh
flowers and dried fish are displayed alongside one
another, mingling their fragrance.

Most colourful are little sacks of spices; and onions with bright purple skins. Betel leaves are counted out for the making of 'pan'. The more daring visitors may want to sample the range of sweets on display, mostly looking home-made. Some are lightly covered in a thin silver foil which is edible.

Historically, Mapusa's Friday market even acted as an informal marriage market where families could look out for prospective marriage partners for their sons or daughters.

Anjuna Beach features a Wednesday handicrafts market popularised by the hippies. But today the selling is done mainly by the Kashmiris who believe in hard-sell of their shawls, carpets and woodcarvings. In strong contrast are the Tibetan traders who display their wares in much more artistic fashion.

However, some flower-power hippies still gather to sell handmade clothing, bags, rugs and jewellery. You can have your ears pierced and your hair cut. It's a fascinating place for people watching, against the background of a most picturesque beach where you can relax or swim after exploring the market.

What to buy

During a holiday in India, you will almost certainly be tempted to buy souvenirs, and possibly more expensive items such as jewellery and furniture.

There is wide choice of local handicrafts made from wood, brass and marble. Beautiful fabrics are made into all kinds of clothing, and there are good bargains in casual wear.

Indian jewellers are highly skilled in silver filigree and heavy gold work.

State-run emporia with fixed prices, or small shops and bazaars where you can barter, are preferable to street pedlars who usually ask at least three times the realistic price.

Beware of being overcharged at tourist shops, and be ready to haggle. 'Walking away tactics' are usually effective in bringing down the price, especially if you start moving towards a neighbouring shop that sells similar products.

Be careful about costly antiques which may not be authentic. Production of antiques is a flourishing cottage industry.

If a shop undertakes to ship bulkier purchases such as rugs, carpets or furniture, the goods will always take far longer to arrive than is promised. You may have to pay duty and VAT when the package arrives. If you anticipate buying costly items, it's worth checking on the levels of import duty payable before leaving the UK.

Jewellery – Hotel shops are the safest place to buy big items. The price may be slightly higher, but jewellers will give a certificate of authenticity.

Fabrics – The bazaars have cheaper prices, but some of the more special weaves are found in the shops.

Saris – Vary in length throughout the country, so check the local length before you have it made up. When fabric is cut from a long continuous piece, it is sold by the metre length, but the width is still described in inches.

Silk – The average price of raw silk is just over £3 per metre. If you are having clothing tailor-made, don't pay until you are satisfied with the product.

T-shirts – Ideal gifts, costing only about £1 each. Available from market and beach vendors, but haggle!

Pottery – Terracotta pots and artefacts are priced from 10 to 350 Rs from any handicraft store. For more artistic pieces, it is worth visiting Kamarkhazana, near Mapusa, where individual designer items are available.

Decorated boxes – Made from papier-mâché, they come in all shapes and sizes, beautifully decorated.

Leather bags – Excellent quality and unique designs. The best are in the hotel shops.

Carpet & rugs – Prices vary according to the material. Silk carpets are the most expensive. The number of knots and the age of the carpet will also determine the price. Again, the best qualities are usually in the hotel shops.

Cashmere – Prices are about one-third those in the UK.

Spices – Ideal for trying out your favourite curries back home. A complete range is available from the markets at Margao and Mapusa; or in neat packages from the model Spice Farm at Khandepar in Ponda District. Consider this basic shopping list of ten best buys:

Black pepper. Red chillies, ground up and stronger than those one buys in UK. Coriander, ground up. Saffron. Cloves. Cinnamon powder and cinnamon sticks. Jeera, normally called cummin. Grated coconut, sun-dried so that it keeps well. Tamarind, to give a sour taste to a dish.

Cashew Nuts – 200-gramme packets make ideal small gifts. Prices depend on the quality. Broken nuts, generally used for cake-making, are the cheapest. Otherwise, cashew nuts are graded according to size – larger ones cost more – but the flavour is just the same. Prices average around £4 a kilo. In Panaji, at least a dozen shops are clustered together, all selling cashew nuts only, in every grade and packet size. Market ladies sell village cashews at three nuts for one rupee.

Wine & feni – Very few people leave Goa without a bottle or two, costing a pound or less, or a little more for whiskies with ambitious brand-names. Port wine is priced from 20 Rs a bottle. The best selections are at bottle stores in towns such as Margao and Panaji.

3.8 Sport and nightlife

Sport and leisure facilities are mostly limited to what is offered by the hotels. Watersports are very limited in Goa, though there is a water sports centre at the Park Plaza Hotel. Likewise there are no public tennis courts or golf clubs.

Among spectator sports, an essential of many festivals is the bullfight called *dhiri*. Much less bloodthirsty than the Spanish version, a *dhiri* is fought between two thoroughbred bulls who lock horns in a test of strength and endurance. There is excitement and gambling among the spectators.

Football v. cricket

Otherwise, the national sport in Goa is football –
unlike the rest of cricket-mad India. That reflects
the Portuguese influence, in contrast to British. It's
said that football is in the blood of Goans, and
music is in their hearts.

Music and folk dancing is the most popular entertainment open to visitors, who will otherwise find
very limited nightlife. There is enormous range of
colourful performances that reflect the cultural diversity of Goa: a full range of classical Hindu music and temple dancing; folk music and dances from
the villages; centuries-old songs, dances and costume direct from Portugal; and a post-Independence
fusion of ethnic and western music.

Some shows are presented on river cruises, as
part of a sightseeing package, with guitars as the
most popular instrument. Others are linked with a
Goan meal in a traditional setting. It all makes a
memorable few hours, with ample opportunity for
flash photography. At most of the shows, an MC
explains the action. For dance-happy spectators,
there's often the chance of trying out steps with the
performers.

3.9 Quick facts, all-India & Goa

Total land area: 1,150,000 sq miles – just over
half the size of Europe, or 1/3 of USA (*Goa: 1,400
sq miles – the size of Cornwall, or Rhode Island*).
Coastline: 4,350 miles (*Goa: 65 miles*).
Natural resources: coal (fourth-largest reserves in
the world), iron ore, manganese, mica, bauxite,
titanium ore, chromite, natural gas, diamonds,
crude oil, limestone (*Goa: iron ore*).
Population: 930 million estimate, growth rate
1.9%. (*Goa: 1.2 million, growing faster through
migration from other States*).
Life expectancy: 57 years male, 59 years female.
Total fertility rate: 3.7 children per woman.
Religion: Hindu 83%, Muslim 11%, Christian 2%,
Sikh 2%. (*Goa: Hindu 60%, Catholic 37%*).
Literacy: male 62%, female 34%. (*Goa: 77%*).

Language: Hindi, English, and 14 other official languages; another 24 languages spoken by at least a million people each. (*Goa: Konkani and Marathi; also English and Portuguese*).

Administrative divisions: 25 States and 7 Union Territories.

Independence: 15 August 1947 from UK (*Goa: 1961 from Portugal, and became the 25th State of the Union on 30 May 1987*).

Legal system: based on English common law.

National holiday: Anniversary of the Proclamation of the Republic, 26 January.

Suffrage: universal at age 18.

India's economy: 67% of India's population are engaged in farming, accounting for 30% of GDP. India is now self-sufficient in food grains and a net agricultural exporter, thanks to improved farming methods and use of new seed varieties. However, the green revolution has still not reached millions of villagers who continue to live in deep poverty.

Manufacture ranges from traditional handicrafts to factory production, much out-dated but with some modernisation and switch to high-tech industries. Business is subject to numerous government controls, though there are moves to liberalisation. Annual growth has averaged 4% to 5% during the past decade, with especially strong growth in services. Ongoing problems include 10% inflation, diminished foreign exchange reserves, and a large national debt.

Chapter Four
Goa sightseeing

4.1 Old Goa

Five miles up the Mandovi River from present-day Panaji, Old Goa once ranked among the wealthiest cities of India. Famed in early Hindu history and legend, Old Goa came under Muslim rule in the late 13th century, and became a major port of departure for Muslim pilgrims from India to Mecca.

But the big turning point came on November 25, 1510, when a Portuguese army under Afonso de Albuquerque conquered the city and massacred all the Muslim inhabitants. In this crucial battle, the Portuguese were very heavily out-numbered. They attributed their victory to divine help. November 25 was the day of St Catherine of Alexandria (famed for her martyrdom on a wheel), so the Portuguese decided their success came from her personal intervention. Hence they gratefully dedicated the Cathedral to St Catherine.

Goa was the first Portuguese territorial possession in Asia. Later it became the capital of all Portuguese territories in the East, with the same civic privileges as Lisbon.

By 1565 the city had become a major trading centre, handling the luxury exchange of goods between West and East – China, Persia and India. This was the age of 'Golden Goa'. Peak prosperity reigned from 1575 to 1625.

The cross followed the flag. From the early 16th century Goa became a Franciscan missionary base. St Francis Xavier came to Goa in 1542 and undertook the training of Jesuit missionaries. Goa became the principal Catholic missionary centre for the East, with jurisdiction over all Portuguese territories beyond the Cape of Good Hope.

In Goa itself, thanks to appropriate support from the Inquisition, inhabitants of the coastal areas were converted to Christianity. With the building of the magnificent Sé Cathedral, the Basilica of Bom Jesus, other churches, convents, colleges, a hospital and a one-acre Palace of the Inquisition, Old Goa was rated as the Rome of the East. Population rose to 200,000.

But the glory faded. The Portuguese came under pressure from the Dutch, British and French. Then followed epidemic and decay. In 1843 the seat of government was finally moved to present-day Panaji. Old Goa was abandoned, and fell into ruins. Only a few villagers now reside in what formerly was the greatest city of Portugal's Asian empire.

Old Goa today offers fascinating sightseeing. The masterpieces of 16th-century Portuguese architecture are well preserved in lonely splendour amid the remains. The body of St Francis Xavier, patron saint of Goa, is enshrined in a carved silver casket in the Basilica.

Certainly no holiday visit is complete without taking in the sights of Old Goa. Sightseeing tours can combine Old Goa with a circuit of the principal Hindu temples; or can be linked with spare time in Panaji, and possibly a sunset river cruise rounded off by a traditional evening meal. There are several options. Ask your rep what's on offer.

From Panaji, the principal approach to Old Goa – also known by its Portuguese name of Velha Goa – is along a 7-mile causeway built by the Portuguese in the 17th century. Formerly the connection between the two cities was by boat. On the left is the River Mandovi; on the right, an area of salt pans, with a few water buffaloes grazing alongside.

It's a beautiful drive, looking across to Chorao Island. Part of that island is dedicated to a bird sanctuary with lush vegetation that encourages coots, grey herons, egrets, kingfishers, brahminy ducks, sandpipers and the migratory pintail. Around 180 species have been recorded.

Along the tidal mudflats some of these birds can be seen from the road. The Portuguese style of villas facing the river are shaded by coconut palms.

The two great monuments of Old Goa – the gleaming-white Cathedral and the reddish-brown Basilica – face one another across a square. The entire green-lawn area is a World Heritage Site. "Anyone who causes damage can get three months in gaol and/or a fine of up to 5,000 Rs."

The Basilica of Bom (Good) Jesus contains the tomb and mortal remains of St Francis Xavier who in 1541 was responsible for spreading Christianity throughout the Portuguese colonies in the East.

The basilica is built on a cruciform plan of red laterite stone, combined with a cement-coloured stone which is schist. Construction took only 11 years, from 1594. The white building alongside is a guest house, with accommodation for the priests.

Inside the basilica, the main features are a 17th-century richly gilded main altar, a statue above of St Ignatius of Loyola (founder of the Jesuit Order), a fantastic pulpit of carved teak, and the Italian silver casket where most of St Francis Xavier is displayed. His right arm is in St Peter's, Rome.

The casket was installed in 1637, but the marble mausoleum – the 10-year work of a Florentine sculptor Giovanni Foggini – was not finished until 1698. The anniversary of the saint's death, December 3, is a public holiday. Every tenth year his casket is lowered for a six-week period, so that pilgrims can have a closer look. The saint's next public appearance is scheduled for the year 2004. Make a note in your diary.

In the annexe, paintings depict scenes from the life of St Francis Xavier, and there's an art gallery upstairs. Birds nest and twitter in the cloisters.

Sé Cathedral is the largest in Asia, built between 1562 and 1652 in Portuguese Gothic style. Originally there were towers each side of the West Door, but one collapsed in 1776. The remaining tower houses a famous bell, often called the Golden Bell because of its rich sound.

Formerly the bell tolled whenever the Inquisition was pronouncing public sentence on heretics and sinners in a solemn ceremony – an *auto-da-fé* ('act of faith'). For those who repented, the judges ordered suitable penance. Obstinate heretics who refused to confess were handed over to the secular authorities for immediate burning at the stake. The bell still rings daily, but not for bonfires.

The cathedral took 90 years to build, from 1562 till 1652. The altar is dedicated to St Catherine of Alexandria. A carving on the bottom row, centre, of the altar depicts the saint with her wheel of martyrdom. The 16th-century organ is played regularly.

One of the side chapels has a baroque entrance gate with intricate carving. Within is a cross which reputedly has healing properties, and is therefore the object of veneration and pilgrimage.

Goa's best examples of Portuguese religious art are in the adjoining convent and church of St Francis of Assisi. Rebuilt from a mosque in 1521, it contains gilded woodcarvings and beautiful murals. The floor is made of carved gravestones. Round the back is an Archaeological Museum.

Of historical interest is the Viceroy's Arch, which celebrates the Portuguese conquest of the city. It was erected by Francisco da Gama, who was the governor from 1597 to 1600. He erected the monument in memory of his great-grandfather, the explorer Vasco da Gama, whose statue looks out to sea. From the neighbouring landing stage, a ferry crosses to Divar Island.

4.2 Temples

The Portuguese occupation of Goa came in two waves. The first four coastal districts to be subdued in the early 16th century were known as the 'Old Conquests' (Velhas Conquistas). Later the Portuguese mastered seven more districts in the hilly inland areas – the 'New Conquests' (Novas Conquistas).

During the first wave, temples were destroyed, to be replaced by churches. Persuasion ensured that most of the occupied population became Christian.

Many Hindus retreated from coastal and river-bank areas to the relative safety of the foothills, where they re-established new shrines and temples, especially in Ponda district.

The pattern has remained into the 20th century. Coastal areas are mainly Catholic, and the interior Hindu. The market town of Ponda is the centre of numerous Hindu shrines. Several of Goa's main temples can easily be visited in a sightseeing tour that includes beautiful scenery and traditional Hindu villages.

Against a lush backdrop of paddy fields, palm trees, woodlands and green hills, the temples add another brilliant touch to the colour scheme. Their architecture is distinctive, with a standard layout to each complex. Outside the main entrance gate is a sacred water tank for ritual bathing. A tall lamp tower called a Dipa-Stambha overlooks the precincts. Guest rooms called Agrashalas for pilgrims are ranged around the inner courtyard.

Shri Manguesh Temple – Along a road towards Ponda, in a beautiful setting of terraced hillsides, coconut palms and mango trees, the temple's elegant white lamp tower stands out on a hilltop. The local village has a serene atmosphere. Meeting the needs of the pilgrim trade which brings thousands of visitors every year, there's a line of souvenir stalls, kiosks, and people selling sun-hats and fruit.

Leading up to the welcome gate, lines of women and children offer lotus garlands for a rupee or two. It's hard to resist hanging some around your neck.

This temple is dedicated to the Goddess Parvati, the heavenly consort of Lord Siva. Like many Hindu temples elsewhere in the territory, Shri Manguesh shows signs of Portuguese influence. The interior, for instance, is fitted with Portuguese chandeliers.

The surrounding courtyard with accommodation for pilgrims looks remarkably like a south-European medieval monastery in plan, colouring and details. The window grilles, for example, are pure Portuguese in style.

35

Shri Shantadurga Temple – Dedicated to the Goddess of Peace, this temple dates from year 1728, and is located at the foothill of Kavalem near Ponda. Every day at one p.m. a religious ceremony is held with the inner shrine illuminated by reflected sunlight, directed by a mirror.

4.3 Panaji

This pleasant whitewashed city on the south bank of the Mandovi River became the Goan capital last century. Many of the building materials were floated down-river from the abandoned city of Old Goa. The town reflects its Portuguese heritage.

The most important monument is the Secretariat building, once a Muslim Palace then a Portuguese Fort. The Portuguese governor-generals moved here from Old Goa in 1760, and it remained their official palace until a royal decree in 1843 also made it the seat of government.

The gleaming white building faces the river, with a few antique cannons as reminder of the historic past. Alongside is a small park that centres on a dramatic statue of the Abbé Faria, who is claimed as the founder of hypnosis by suggestion. He was born 1756, and died in Paris 1819. He was immortalised in the novel by Alexandre Dumas, *The Count of Monte Cristo*.

A stroll along the quayside towards the river mouth takes one past several pleasure boats that offer afternoon and evening cruises with Goan folk entertainment. Fishing boats cluster together, and there's the constant sight of rusty barges, laden with iron ore for international export through Mormugao.

A crowded but minimum-cost ferry operates a regular service across the river, but there are two bridges just a mile or two upstream. Previously there was one newly-built bridge which fell down. Now they have two bridges side by side, presumably 'just in case'. These bridges are the only direct road link between north and south Goa.

The best view over the city's red-tiled rooftops is from the Altinho hill above Panaji, where delightful houses and gardens are located.

A focal point of the city centre is the 16th-century Church of the Immaculate Conception, a dazzling white cathedral which stands out beautifully against the skyline, with a dramatic stairway to the entrance.

As Goa's commercial and administrative centre, Panaji also features shops that are well stocked with a wide selection of local products. Much of the original Portuguese character still remains, including numerous low-life taverns.

Although English has virtually taken over, some shop signs still cling to their Portuguese fascia boards. You can choose, for instance, between the Berberia Real (Royal Barber Shop) and a rival called the Friends Haircutting Saloon.

4.4 Countryside, crops and spices

One of the pleasures of Goa is the ease of seeing first-hand the life of village India, which often is only a few minutes' walk from your resort hotel.

On sightseeing excursions to markets, churches or temples, the cross-country journeys are packed with still more interest: an ever-changing panorama of village scenes, people, farming and gorgeous scenery.

It's possible to dig deeper, taking a closer look at rural India than is possible from behind an air-conditioned window. There are jeep safaris available, short on comfort but long on atmosphere. You can explore little dirt tracks where no other westerners go, and then finally arrive at a beach where the jeep party is totally on its own.

Another option is based on a demonstration of country crafts such as processing the rice harvest, or watching toddy tappers at work (see page 39), or seeing how spices are grown. Some of these tours are rounded out with an ethnic meal, or folk music and dance performances.

There's much more to rural Goa than subsistence farming. Employment patterns are changing as more people move away from traditional fishing, farming, forestry and mining in favour of the service industries, especially tourism. Eleven small industrial estates have been established near villages, to foster small manufacture and labour-intensive cottage industries. High educational standards in Goa – second only to Kerala in literacy rating – makes it easier for Goans to learn new skills.

The villages themselves have great charm, normally focussing either on a whitewashed church or a multi-coloured Hindu temple. Virtually every village house has a kitchen garden that grows vegetables such as okra, capsicum, chillies, aubergines, garlic and pumpkins. The yellow pumpkin flowers are also chopped into a vegetable. Country chickens wander around, free-range.

Flowers are everywhere, with bougainvillaea rampant. Women and schoolgirls walk along with a single flower in their hair or garlands of lotus blossoms.

Useful trees border the villages: tamarind, jackfruit, mango and papaya. At village ponds, water buffaloes come for a drink with egrets in close attendance, while kingfishers flit amid the water lilies. Everything is green, thanks to the torrential rains of June till late September. In flat areas, rice paddies are backed by coconut groves.

Generally, rice is a once-a-year crop, raised during the monsoon months. With irrigation two crops are possible. On some terraced fields they plant okra and cucumbers during the monsoon.

Plots which are used for rice paddies during the rains are planted with green vegetables and beans after the harvest. These crops need less moisture, and grow well during the remainder of the year.

The hills are a beautiful feature of Goa, with winding roads and lush green foliage. Many slopes are terraced, or planted with fruit trees. Here and there the reddish laterite rock is quarried, and cut into blocks for house construction. A tougher form of this laterite was used in building the Basilica and other monuments in Old Goa. The colouring is a reminder that Goa's most lucrative export is iron ore, delivered in huge quantities especially to Japan.

Even the steepest hills can support plantations of fruit and nut trees. Typical are the 50-ft betel nut trees, with pineapples growing in their shade.

Betel-chewing

From the totally different betel vine comes the small leaves that are used as an envelope for 'pan', a paste of betel nut, lime and spices. Pan is chewed after meals as a digestive aid and breath sweetener, causing a brick-red saliva which stains the lips, mouth and gums. This betel-chewing custom is spread widely throughout India.

Villagers take pride in their mangoes, which are very high in sugars. In the heat of May, when mangoes are fully ripe, they can rot in three days. The Goans gorge themselves during that harvest season, but also produce large quantities of mango juice as a year-round thirst-quencher. They convert surplus mangoes into chutney or jam.

The most interesting fruit is the cashew, "the money plant of Goa". Cashew nuts are Goa's leading cash crop and currency earner. The trees were originally introduced by the Portuguese to halt erosion on hillsides which were useless for rice terracing. Once the trees are planted, they need very little attention. There is enough monsoon rain to ensure ideal growing conditions.

The fruit itself is roughly pear-shaped, but smaller, while the nut hangs down *outside* the fruit – a unique arrangement! There's no need to climb the trees for harvesting during the February to May season. Villagers wait until the red and yellow fruits actually drop – when fully ripe – and merely have to pick them up. Apart from domestic use, the cashew nuts go to factories for processing, ready for local sale and export.

The cashew fruit is dripping with juice. Open it with care, otherwise your clothes will be drenched! It has a reasonable flavour, and smells rather like mango. Some attempts have been made to bottle the juice, but it has not taken off in popularity. Instead it is used as a base for the alcohol called feni.

Villagers tread the semi-liquid pulp in traditional style, and store the juice in barrels for a few days' natural fermentation. The wine-like liquid is then poured into earthenware pots, and a fire lit underneath. Through a primitive pipe, distilled alcohol drips into a smaller vessel. In this raw state, the cashew urrack is a popular village drink. Otherwise the product is sold to bottling plants for a second distillation, to produce a smoother feni that sells in liquor shops for 50 or 60 Rs per bottle.

A similar product is coconut-palm feni made from distilled toddy. With Goa's large plantations of coconut trees, toddy-tapping can be almost a full-time job. Men climb the coconut palms barefoot, using the tree rings as a toe-hold.

The sweet colourless sap can be an instant thirst-quencher, or allowed to ferment into a low-alcohol beverage, or distilled into a straight liquor.

Formerly, toddy was used in bread-making, because it was high in yeast. But that use has now discontinued. Toddy vinegar, however, is still an essential part of the Goan kitchen – used in vindalho dishes, for instance.

Model spice farm

An award-winning spice and fruit farm at Khandepar in Ponda District is open to visitors. It's a man-made Garden of Eden, except for no apple trees. In this model 50-acre farm, the owners have planted specimens of every fruit or spice-bearing tree or shrub grown in Goa and neighbouring states.

Ornamental plants also have been given space. Experiments and techniques used on the estate attract study groups of farmers, who also take home saplings and cuttings of new varieties.

Typically, the owners use organic methods to produce an average yield per tree of 120 coconuts a year compared with the Goan average of 80. Dwarf trees, with smaller nuts, yield 250 compared with the State average of 140.

Interplanting with spice trees and bushes is another key to improved land use, though many of the spices are normally field crops. You can see first-hand how some well-known spices are grown and processed.

Cloves grow best in Kerala, which supplies 90% of India's total production. Goan climate is not moist enough in comparison with Kerala, which gets much more rain.

Nutmeg trees likewise grow better in the moister conditions of Kerala. Trees are eight years old before starting to yield a crop. When mature, a tree bears over 1,000 nuts per year.

Cinnamon is one of the easiest trees to grow. Stick a cutting in the ground, and a year later it has flourished and the bark is ready for harvesting in the form of cinnamon sticks.

Black Pepper grows on vines which cling to coconut trees, so that two crops come from the same piece of ground. Each vine yields 1½ kilos of black pepper. The vine is similar to the one producing betel leaves.

All-spice trees are native to Kerala, but are being grown in Goa as an experiment. The berries give some of the aroma and flavour of all spices.

4.5 Birdlife

There are 250 breeds of birds in Goa, of which an alert bird-watcher should spot at least fifty during a holiday. Even for a less dedicated enthusiast, it's worth packing binoculars for the added pleasure of taking a closer look at Goa's birdlife. Here are some birds to expect.

Black drongo or **king crow** – is the one with very long, deeply forked tail, likes perching on telephone lines.
Blue-tailed bee-eater – seen at the edge of the beach.
Brahminy kite – very common, scavenging around lakes and villages, very distinctive when in flight.
Brown-headed gull – looks like a blackheaded gull but is bigger.
Cattle egrets – snow-white birds, usually standing on or near cattle to feed on insects.
Chiffchaff – same as the British bird.
Common sandpiper – wades in rock pools.
Common iora – greenish or yellow-green plumage.
Coucal – lives in shrubs and on the ground.
Golden oriole – We always think it's wonderful to see one in Britain, but here they are hanging off every tree.

Hooded crows – unwanted, and unloved.

House sparrows – the first birds you see on landing at the airport.

Indian robin – black with a red band.

Koel – goes whoop-whoop-whoop.

Large pied wagtail – seen around flowing water, and takes rides on river ferry-boats.

Lesser golden-backed woodpecker – bright golden-yellow and black, with red crest.

Little stint – seen on the beach.

Little egret – has yellow feet and black bill, living at water's edge.

Magpie-robin – looks like a miniature magpie but its tail is cocked up. A good singer.

Mynah – several varieties, usually seen in small groups, flying between palm trees, occasionally perched high.

Paddy bird or **pond heron** – difficult to see when settled, but easily spotted in flight due to the flash of its distinctive white wings.

Pariah kites – dark brown plumage, forked tail easily seen in flight.

Plovers – lots of golden plovers, and parties of about a hundred little sand plovers in a field.

Purple-rumped sunbird – black or brown above, yellow below.

Ruff-dove – looks like a British pigeon.

Rufous-backed shrike – watches its territory from a conspicuous perch.

Spotted dove – recognised by white-spotted black collar.

White-breasted kingfisher – usually seen by hotel pools, catching fish and insects, and is happy on lawns.

White-backed munia – about the size of a black-bird, and is half-black and half-white down its chest.

White-browed bulbul and **redvented bulbul** – cheerful and noisy, always chattering.

Yellow-cheeked tit – has a black crest.

Chapter Five

Food and drink

5.1 Goan cuisine

Thanks to former occupations by Muslims and Portuguese, Goa offers a wide range of cuisine that includes Indian, Goan, Portuguese, Chinese, vegetarian and non-vegetarian.

In major hotels and restaurants, a choice of cuisines is offered, but of course the chefs have more skill in cooking their familiar local dishes. Part of the holiday experience is to sample the full flavour of Goan cuisine.

Outside the hotels, Goa has relatively few first-class eating places. However, most beaches feature very basic shack restaurants which offer refreshments, snacks, Goan dishes and seafood.

They are much cheaper than the hotels, but their standards of hygiene are dubious in the absence of running water or adequate toilet facilities.

We suggest you try the hotel dining rooms before venturing to eat outside. Hotel kitchen standards are now generally fairly high. But in rural districts or shack restaurants beware of salads, raw vegetables and soft fruits.

South Indian food is hotter than in northern India, and leans much more towards vegetarian dishes, using grains and lentils besides the staple rice. However, some Indian vegetarians eat seafood, on the basis that fish is 'fruit of the sea'.

Goan food in hotels is normally served medium spiced – enough to make them interesting, but not so hot as in home cooking. The scarlet chillies are cooled down by adding more coconut.

Ethnic tableware

To be completely authentic, Goan food is served on banana leaf plates, with coconut utensils. If you go all the way and eat with your fingers, remember that only the right hand should be used for putting food in your mouth. In the Indian culture, the left hand is reserved for other bodily needs.

Goans are specially fond of seafood which is prepared by different communities in different ways. According to a typical menu, seafood is supplied "Fresh with the spirit of the ocean." Prices depend on season and size. You can choose to have your fish fried with granulated rice, with masala gravy, stuffed or tandoori.

Some of the local fish names are not recognised by an English dictionary, and it's hard to find exact translations of seafood such as chomak, raons, modso or muddoshyo (lady fish). But one can feel amid more familiar territory when there's mackerel on the menu, or sardines, kingfish, grouper, squid, mullet and the well-known shellfish.

The temptation with shellfish is that it's so fresh and plentiful that it's easy to over-indulge. At a shack restaurant, prawns with rice may possibly cost only 30 Rs. In a well-known Panaji restaurant, a Prawn Sukem costing 70 Rs is billed as a spicy mixture of prawns with onions and coconut.

Vegetarian dishes are hot and non-greasy, very tasty when enlivened with freshly ground spices. Curries are varied in content and strength but always fried in ghee (a kind of clarified butter) and served with rice. Side helpings of dal (pulses), pickles or curd-based dishes help soothe the palate.

Biryani is the generic name for numerous dishes based on fried rice – also known as pulav – often flavoured or coloured with turmeric or saffron. There are chicken biryanis, mutton, prawns, or vegetable.

India generally is no place for a dedicated meat-lover, and Goa is no exception. It's much better to stay with fish. However, something unusual for India is that Goan Christians eat numerous pork dishes, many disguised as sausages. That could be the main Portuguese contribution to the Goan menu.

Baker's basket

Breads are available in great variety. Bakers start selling bread from 5 a.m., with baskets strapped to their bicycles. They announce their arrival by sounding a horn. Their stock normally includes:

Kankonn – Hard crisp bread shaped like a bangle, and usually dipped in one's morning tea.
Poie – A thick chapati-type bread that can be halved, to be stuffed with meat or vegetables.
Sanna – Steamed rice bread steeped in coconut toddy, with a sweetish taste. Can be eaten alone, or dipped in gravy.
Unde – Crusted round bread with a slit on top.

Breakfast dishes

An effective way to counteract digestive problems is to start each day with some natural yoghourt (sometimes known as 'cura'). Other breakfast specialities include 'idlis' (steamed rice dumplings), vadais (deep-fried savoury doughnuts) and dosais (wafer-thin rice pancakes). They each come in dozens of varieties and flavours. Masala dosais, for instance, are filled with a spicy mixture of potatoes fried with onion.

5.2 Goan menus

To help you interpret Goan menus, with some clue to the ingredients, here are some guidelines.

Ambot Tik – A sour and pungent paste usually stuffed into shark, squid, electric ray or catfish. It is one of the few preparations made without coconut, and is best served with rice.
Chicken or mutton do piaza – Cooked in gravy with lots of onions.
Chicken Cajreal – Chicken marinated in a preparation of chillies, ginger, garlic and lime. Grilled, roasted or griddled, it is served with a salad and squeezed lime.
Chourisso – Spicy pork sausages, either boiled or fried with onions and chillies.
Dal – A lentil dish best tried with nan bread or chapatis.

Feijuado – A special sauce added to dry beans and local sausages.

Khatkhate – Diced bananas, sweet potatoes, pumpkins and carrots, cooked in a masala made of coconut.

Masala – A paste, such as ground chillies, with some sugar and toddy vinegar – added to a variety of dishes.

Mergolho – Prepared from pumpkin and papaya, cooked in coconut juice and milk masala.

Paneer steak – Cottage cheese steak grilled and served with curried sauce and rice.

Sorpotel – Diced pork liver, well fried and cooked in a toddy vinegar, medium spicy.

Vindalho – A pungent dish made of diced beef, pork or fish, added to a gravy with a base of garlic and a rich helping of toddy vinegar.

Xacuti – A preparation of coconut juice, grated and roasted coconut, and a variety of roasted spices, usually added to mutton.

Xec Xec – pronounced shek shek. A tasty crab dish made with grated coconut, garlic and ginger.

Desserts which are predominantly sweet:

Bebinca – A multi-layered coconut cake made from flour, egg yolks, sugar, coconut juice and nutmeg.

Bolinhas – small round cakes made of coconut and semolina, topped with a cherry.

Dodol – Rich in taste and made with jaggery (a coarse brown sugar made from the sap of date palms) coconut juice and nuts.

Neureos – Made of a paste of dough, stuffed with a mixture of grated coconut, cardamon seeds, sugar, nuts and raisins.

Perada – A guava cheese made either hard, or soft and sticky. Looks like solid treacle, and is very sweet.

5.3 All the drinks

The rule 'don't drink the tap water' applies rigidly in the Indian sub-continent. Jugs of purified water are supplied in hotel rooms, and tea, coffee and soft drinks are safe. But remember that the ice cubes in drinks outside your hotel could be made from unpurified water. 'When in doubt leave it out'.

Bottled mineral water is available, costing 10 Rs a litre in supermarkets, and somewhat more in hotels and restaurants. A popular brand in Goa is called Bailley's. It's worth packing a vacuum flask, to keep the liquid cool during day trips.

Fresh fruit juices are sold everywhere from wayside kiosks, amd you may wish to try neera – coconut juice, good after too much of the local hooch called feni.

An especially refreshing drink is freshly squeezed lime juice and soda, with or without sugar. Buttermilk is also a tasty thirst quencher. Another local favourite is Lassi, a yoghourt based drink. Besides tasting good, it's an excellent stomach settler should you have any problems.

At most places of interest, vendors sell factory-bottled soft drinks. These are quite safe, but it's a good idea to carry some drinking straws with you, to avoid using some of the dubious drinking containers offered.

Popular brands are: Miranda (orange); Limca (bitter lemon); Citra (7-Up); and Thums Up (local Cola).

Some shack restaurants and refreshment kiosks offer sugar cane drinks, based on freshly mangled cane. In some places the vendors have moved into the 20th century with power-driven presses.

In contrast to the rest of India, commercially produced alcoholic drinks are freely sold in Goa at very reasonable prices in bottle stores. Dry white wines cost 55 Rs a bottle; sweet port wines – a Portuguese legacy – cost between 25 and 40 Rs.

In hotel bars and restaurants, Kingfisher beer or an Arlem Pilsner cost about 30 Rs for a 60-cc bottle; whisky and gin 25 Rs a 30-ml tot; small glasses of Golconda dry white wine for 15 Rs.

Everywhere in Goa you'll see advertisements for whisky, which mostly is produced in the neighbouring State of Karnataka. Typical brand-names are

Black Knight, Director's Special, Black Stallion, Officers' Choice, Diplomat, Aristocrat, Royal Velvet and Royal Challenge.

These drinks mostly cost only 80 Rs a bottle in liquor stores, or 5 Rs for a 30-ml tot in a wayside bar plus another 3 Rs for soda. On a scale of ten for Scotch, connoisseurs rate Indian whisky around four. Local rum, vodka and gin are rated higher.

The Goans also produce their own local liquor – feni – distilled either from palm toddy or from cashew fruit. Feni tastes rather like raw slivovitz. Take a quick gulp, and it's like being shot in the throat. But double distilled feni, flavoured with cummin seeds or ginger, is much smoother. (See the previous chapter for more information on this popular village industry).

5.4 Fruits

Depending on the season, Goa offers a year-round supply of fruits: water melons, grapefruit, mangoes, pineapples, jackfruits, papayas, guavas, bananas, grapes and even a few custard apples (a fruit eaten with a spoon).

Beware of eating fruit which cannot be peeled.

Main picture: Deserted beach in Sri Lanka
Top Left: Sri Lankan ladies picking tea
Bottom right: Stunning sunsets in Sri Lanka

The magnificent Taj Mahal, Agra

Beautiful beaches in Goa

Sinhalese frescoes, Sri Lanka

Island resort, Maldives

Indian woman with child

Chapter Six

The northern highlights

6.1 Delhi and the Golden Triangle

Delhi is India's richest city in sightseeing potential and is the prime base for side trips to Agra and Jaipur – the so-called 'Golden Triangle'.

From south to north through the sprawling capital – now with 9 million population – historians and archaeologists count seven or eight distinct cities built by successive rulers. The first city was established around 1060 AD, though there is evidence of continuous settlement from the 3rd century BC. The great monuments range from the early Moslem period of 12th century onwards, through Moghul period (1526-1857), and thence to the buildings of modern Delhi.

A series of broad, tree-lined avenues and parks separates the teeming bazaars, temples and mosques of Old Delhi from the British-built administrative capital of New Delhi, with its India Gate memorial, government ministries, embassies and modern hotels in garden settings.

City tours are normally split to give half-day each for New and Old Delhi. Sightseeing of New Delhi is combined with many ancient remains including Jantar Mantar, the Qutb Minar and Humayun's Tomb.

Surrounded by ultra-modern office blocks, **Jantar Mantar** is a fantastic astronomical observatory built in 1724 during the reign of Maharajah Jai Singh II of Jaipur (1699-1743). He took a keen interest in astronomy, both eastern and western, and built similar structures at Jaipur and Varanasi. The red

stone 'instruments' look like surrealistic sculptures, with graduated markings to take readings. The centrepiece is a sun-dial, 40 ft high.

A truly more modern sightseeing highlight – west of the central area of Connaught Place – is the **Lakshmi Narayan Temple**, a colourful Hindu temple built in 1938. It is often called **Birla Temple**, after the philanthropist who financed the building.

Humayun's Tomb, built 1565, is the first major example of Mughal architecture, with an octagonal ground plan, lofty arches, pillared kiosks and a double dome. These details became a prototype for the Taj Mahal in Agra. There are rich photo opportunities, such as pictures of bullocks that power the lawnmowers. Visitors are waylaid by women with pots on their heads, all ready to pose for a modelling fee of five rupees. Snake-charmers tune up whenever a Westerner approaches.

The **Qutb Minar** is the tallest stone tower in India – a 13th-century landmark 240 ft high, visible for miles. The fluted minaret tapers gracefully from a base of 47 feet diameter to the summit which is a slender 8 feet.

Alongside the Qutb Minar is India's earliest surviving mosque, which translates as **The Might of Islam Mosque**. Completed in 1197, it was greatly enlarged by later rulers. Twenty-seven Jain and Hindu temples were demolished to provide building materials. The carved decorations blend Islamic and Hindu traditions.

A famous 5th-century **Iron Pillar** in the mosque courtyard shows not a trace of rust – a tribute to the skill of ancient India's metalworkers. By tradition, anyone who can reach backwards to clasp hands around the pillar will have good luck.

Old Delhi

The 7th city dates from 1638 when the Emperor Shah Jahan moved his capital from Agra back to Delhi. Former cities were demolished to build the magnificent red sandstone fort and extend the city walls to a circumference of over five miles. Five of the fourteen huge entrance gates still remain: Delhi Gate, Kashmiri, Turkman, Ajmeri and Lahori.

The Red Fort

Virtually a town in itself, the Fort covers a very large area. Some parts of the grounds are still fenced off as a military area. Deeper into the Fort, you pass through a gateway where tickets are sold for Sound and Light Shows. Be sure to return after dark for a staging of the great historical events that took place within the citadel walls.

In contrast to the teeming highways outside, the Fort is a delightful haven of tranquillity. The buildings are low profile, most of them glistening white, set around green lawns bordered by floral displays. Indian women tourists themselves add a rich colour to the scene, with their flowing saris.

The palaces of the inner courtyard provide excellent perching and nesting places for the resident birdlife, like a gigantic aviary. From the palace balconies one can look down on snake-charmers who hope that coins and banknotes will flutter down in appreciation of the music and the swaying snakes.

Chandni Chowk

The historic Main Street of Old Delhi is a ceremonial avenue widened during Shah Jahan's reign for his glittering processions to Red Fort. In 17th century it became a street of great houses, jewellers and cloth merchants, who gave it a long-standing reputation as the world's richest thoroughfare. Today, the Imperial glory and wealth have gone, but the area remains rich in interest.

Much city life is lived in the open. Chapati sellers are surrounded by customers eating the pancake-style bread hot from the griddle. Men and children wash at street standpipes; barbers and their clients squat for an open-air shave; nimble-fingered flower sellers string garlands of blooms; cycle repairers festoon tree branches with tubes and tyres.

Virtually any time of the day, Chandni Chowk is totally clogged with cycle rickshaws, scooter-taxis, horse-drawn tongas, bullock-carts, gaily-painted trucks, taxis and private cars. Through the jam move the myriad, colourful characters of India – men pushing hand-carts; a one-stringed fiddle

salesman, with day's stock balanced on his head as
he walks along playing; the fortune-tellers, holy
men, beggars, porters and countrymen.

Almost opposite the Red Fort is another of Shah
Jahan's great buildings – the **Jama Masjid**, the
largest and most beautiful mosque in India. Admis-
sion for non-Muslims is permitted every morning
until noon, and from 14-16 hrs.

Further out past the Kashmiri Gate, the Grand
Trunk Road leads to a 14th-century fortress area
called **Feroz Shah Kotlah** – the historic fifth city
of Delhi – famed for the 27-ton **Ashoka Pillar**
dragged from 125 miles away. The pillar dates
from 3rd century BC.

Shopping
Really determined shoppers could go bargain-hunt-
ing in Chandni Chowk, especially if they have well-
sharpened haggling skills. Otherwise, Connaught
Place and Connaught Circus (now renamed Indira
Ghandi Chowk) in New Delhi offer a complete
range of Indian products, with honest shipping by
reputable firms. Even so, some bargaining is still
necessary, except in the various State Industries
Emporia which operate on a strictly fixed-price
basis. Highly recommended is the Central Cottage
Industries Emporium in Janpath.

6.2 Agra

Agra has far more to offer than just the Taj Mahal.
Seat of the Moghul Emperors during 16th and 17th
centuries, Agra rivals Delhi for historical background and awe-inspiring monuments; a great red-
sandstone **Fort** with walls 1.5 miles around; palaces, mosques and royal tombs lavishly built with
glistening white marble, and a fantastic wealth of
inlay work with precious and semi-precious stones.

Although the **Taj Mahal** is totally familiar to
most travellers, thanks to photos and paintings that
make the royal tomb into one of the world's best-
known monuments, the impact is still breathtaking.

Through a massive gateway, 100 ft high, the
visitor gets his first view of the mausoleum that

took 20,000 labourers and craftsmen 12 years to complete. Whether seen in daytime or by full moon, the Taj Mahal ranks as India's most fabulous sight.

Certainly Shah Jahan kept his vow to build the greatest memorial that the world had ever seen, in memory of his beloved wife Mumtaz Mahal, who gave him 14 children and then died in childbirth.

Outside the standard sightseeing circuit, there's great interest in visiting workshops where craftsmen still produce marble inlay and mosaic, using all the patience, skill and primitive-looking tools that built the Taj Mahal.

Evenings? It's worth taking a slow-paced ride around Agra, through shopping areas where stall-holders sit patiently cross-legged, listening to their radios and cassette-players. By the light of pressure lamps, food vendors prepare variegated stews, fried dishes and rice. With any luck, there'll be a joyous, noisy wedding procession. It's a reminder that Agra is much more than a city of monumental tombs!

6.3 Fatehpur Sikri

Some 24 miles west of Agra, en route to Jaipur, is the 16th-century ghost capital of Fatehpur Sikri. The entire red-sandstone city was built in a six-year period, 1569-1575, during Emperor Akbar's reign.

Nearly seven miles in circumference, the city featured a magnificent mosque and all the necessary buildings for a major palace: a Treasury, Mint, stables, audience halls, sleeping apartments, and even a group of rooms and passages where the Emperor could play hide-and-seek or blind-man's-buff with his court ladies. For another favourite game, the main courtyard was marked out in chess-board style, using dancing girls as live pieces.

An artificial lake was dug out, there were numerous wells and baths and variegated water works. The only snag was that the entire complex had to be abandoned within 14 years owing to failure of the water supply. Today, the perfectly preserved city gives an unforgettable impression of an Emperor's lifestyle of 400 years ago.

6.4 Jaipur

Jaipur, 190 miles from Delhi, is one of India's most beautiful cities, with fine parks and gardens in the best Technicolor tradition. Except for the blue sky, everything is rose-pink. Even the villagers go cycling along in bright pink turbans.

Jaipur was laid out in city-grid blocks by its founder, Maharajah Jai Singh, in 1727. Main streets are precisely 110 feet wide, side streets 55 feet. The entire city is surrounded by a wall of pink sandstone, with eight main gates.

Camels lope in from the surrounding desert. At the main city crossroads, flower-sellers offer gorgeous garlands of stringed marigolds. Close by, the honeycomb facade of the **Palace of the Winds (Hawa Mahal)** has all the most delicate fantasy of the East. It's a favourite photo subject.

The **City Palace** occupies one-seventh of the original walled area of Jaipur, with beautiful gardens and pleasure grounds. The main palace building is the 7-storey **Chandra Mahal**, which offers superb views from the top floor. Also within the grounds is **Jai Singh's Observatory**, which is even more ambitious than his Jantar Mantar in Delhi. The sun-dial is accurate to within two seconds.

Seven miles out of town is **Amber Palace**, the hill-top fortress residence of the Rajput kings for 600 years. At the foot of the steep hillside, modern visitors have the option of changing onto elephants for the last uphill half-mile into the Palace.

Thus the traveller can savour the great highlight of Indian tourism: clutching at the *howdah* rail as the elephant lurches through tall gateways and into the vast palace courtyard. It's really something to write home about: "Travelling like a maharajah!"

The Ganesh Pol gate leads into an inner court where the royal apartments look onto an ornamental garden. Ceilings and walls are covered in delicate mosaics and glass inlays. There are marble screens, and doors inlaid with ivory and sandalwood. That craftsmanship still flourishes in the Jaipur bazaars, famed throughout India for jewellery and gem-stones. If you really know emeralds, buy in Jaipur.

6.5 Udaipur

Like many other Indian cities, the origins of Udaipur are wrapped in legend. The story goes that Maharana Udai Singh was out hunting when he met a holy man on the shores of Lake Pichola. The *sadhu* persuaded the prince to build a new capital city on the site.

Udai Singh duly followed the advice. He began building the walled city of Udaipur in 1559, and then moved away from the ancient Rajput capital of Chitorgarh.

Several artificial irrigation lakes provide an idyllic setting for the palaces, temples and public buildings on which successive rulers lavished their wealth. The entire location is superb, with the lakes set amid green hills.

Standing on a high ridge that runs parallel above Lake Pichola, the marble and granite **City Palace** – also known as the **Maharana's Palace** – is among the largest in Rajasthan. Within the complex are palatial museum apartments gloriously decorated with peacock mosaics, inlaid Chinese tiles and glass craftsmanship.

Lake palaces

Pichola Lake, four square miles in area, was created in the late 14th century. Centred in the lake is the snow-white marble **Jag Nivas Palace**, built in 1757 and then enlarged by later rulers. Today, tourism is king, and the building has been converted to a hotel.

Yet another island palace is **Jag Mandir**, at the southern end of Pichola Lake. The yellow sandstone building, lined with marble inside, was the refuge of Prince Khurram when he was in revolt against his father.

The Prince later achieved his ambitions and became the Emperor Shah Jahan, the builder of the Taj Mahal and other monuments in Agra.

High among the temples of Udaipur is the 80-ft **Jagdish Temple**, perched upon a rectangular platform up a wide flight of steps.

Dedicated to Vishnu, Lord of the Universe, the Jagdish Temple was built in mid-17th century, and is the largest in Udaipur. Elephant carvings decorate the outside walls. The temple's elevated position ensures a wide view over the city.

A canal connects Lake Pichola to **Lake Fateh Sagar** – another of the man-made irrigation lakes which are so necessary for Rajasthan. About 1.5 miles long and a mile wide, the lake view is beautified by hills on three sides.

As for other such lakes in the region, the Rajputs welcomed still more opportunities to enhance the surroundings. Below the lake embankment is **Sahelion Ki Bari** – Garden of the Maids of Honour, who were a present from the Emperor of Delhi to Maharana Sangram Singh II. The park is embellished with an ornamental lotus pond, marble elephants, splendid fountains and finely carved sculptures in black stone.

Treasures of craftsmanship

Like everywhere else in India, there is a rich local tradition of folk art and craftsmanship. A wide collection of folk costumes, ornaments, masks, puppets, dolls, musical instruments and paintings is displayed in the museum called **Bhartiya Lok Kala Mandir**. The museum is deeply involved with the revival of traditional puppet-making and puppet shows. There are daily performances.

Otherwise, a visit can focus the mind on what shopping mementoes to acquire, such as batik wall-hangings, hand-printed textiles, wooden toys, metal sculptures – and puppets!

Thirteen miles north of Udaipur is the **Temple of Eklingji**, founded in 734 AD, but with most of the white marble and sandstone structure dating from late 15th century. Here the investiture ceremonies of the ruling Maharanas were held.

Another mile away is Nagda, where an ancient palace from the 6th century was left in ruins after numerous Muslim invasions. But the main attractions are the **Sas-Bahu Temples** which date from the 11th century. The sculptures and carvings are magnificent, rated among the finest in India.

6.6 Bombay

To experience a total contrast to Goa, Bombay is only a one-hour flight away. Now renamed as Mumbai, it is the second most crowded city of India, after Calcutta. Obviously the shopping potential is far greater than in Goa; and there are major points of sightseeing interest.

Among the most famous monuments is the **Gateway of India** – built 1911 in 16th-century style to commemorate a visit by King George V and Queen Mary. Departure point for launches to Elephanta Island, the area is thronged with peddlers, snake-charmers and fruit-juice vendors.

Between the Gateway and Marine Drive is the heart of business India, which looks more like high-rise Manhattan. **Marine Drive** faces the Arabian Sea with prestige apartments and a green area of sport clubs where cricket is the big game.

Eveningtime, the Marine Drive is a favourite promenade for Bombay families, enjoying the sea breeze. **Chowpatty Beach** – almost deserted during daytime – springs into lively activity at sunset.

Close by, the **Aquarium** displays India's finest collection of tropical marine and fresh-water fish. **Jain Temple**, on top of Malabar Hill, gives a magnificent overall view of Bombay. Close by are the **Hanging Gardens**, built over a water reservoir, and the attractive **Kamala Nehru Children's Park**.

Mani Bhavan is the Mahatma Ghandi Memorial Museum in a house where India's political leader stayed frequently. The **Prince of Wales Museum**, founded 1905, houses one of India's finest collections of coins, miniatures, Nepalese art, antique firearms, archaeology and natural history.

Bombay's most popular excursion is by launch, six miles out of the harbour to Elephanta Island, where mangrove trees fringe the shallow waters. A long flight of steps from the landing-stage reaches to the **Elephanta Caves**, where 7th-century rock-cut temples are dedicated to Lord Shiva. He is depicted as Creator, Protector and Destroyer. A visit gives a crash course in Hindu art, sculpture and mythology.

Chapter Seven

South India experience

7.1 Madras – gateway to the South

With nearly four million population in its metropolitan area of 30 square miles, Madras is the capital and main harbour of Tamil Nadu state.

Broad tree-lined avenues lead from the bustling shopping areas of downtown Madras to modern industrial suburbs engaged in light engineering, textiles and leather manufacture. In movie-making, Madras is a rival to Bombay.

The fourth largest city of India, Madras is much less troubled by the poverty which disturbs visitors to Bombay, Calcutta and parts of Old Delhi.

Madras is a main gateway for South India, which is quite separate in character from Northern India. The South has always been well protected by distance, thick forests and difficult mountain terrain from northern invaders. Hence an untroubled 2,500 years in which the Hindu way of life has flowed almost undisturbed.

While North India is famed for its beautiful Moghul tombs, South India is the land of magnificent temples. With its continuous tradition of customs, music, dance, art and architecture, South India offers the foreign visitor a totally different experience.

Music and dance owe much to Brahmin culture. The classical dance style is called Bharata Natyam, usually performed by a woman, and features graceful statuesque poses to the spellbinding rhythm of Karnatic music.

On the west coast, a popular folk dance is the highly colourful and vigorous Kathakali, performed by masked men to portray the myth and legend of gods, heroes, demons and fabulous beasts.

South India is the home of vegetarian cuisine – highly-spiced dishes that ideally are set out on a banana leaf, used as a disposable dinner plate. One leaf can be cut into five or six dinner plates.

As part of the South India experience, a visitor should certainly sample the vegetarian cuisine – preferably with a local person to explain the ingredients of each dish.

A typical vegetarian lunch could start with an extremely sweet dish called Gulab Jamun (like a small fried dumpling soaked in syrup); then tomato soup followed by a segmented metal platter called *thali* with nine different items, all highly spiced and guaranteed to wake up the jaded palate.

In the fruit, flower and vegetable market of central Madras, all the main ingredients of a South Indian curry are displayed: green peppers, dried red chillies, ginger, grated coconut, garlic, mint and coriander leaves, turmeric, four kinds of lentils, tamarind, bay leaves, clover, cardamom and other spices. An idea of how curry is made can give a keener interest in Indian food - much better than just dismissing it as "Too hot!"

Of lively human interest is the flower section of the market, where blossoms are sold wholesale or retail by weight, or ready knotted into garlands of oleander flowers, jasmine, roses, chrysanthemums, marigolds, couch-flower, iris and lotus buds.

Most South Indian girls and women wear garlands in their glossy black hair. The flowers or buds are knotted two at a time on a strand of banana fibre, often with the inclusion of sweet-smelling herbs. Garland-making skills are learned in childhood, along with how to make a good curry.

City sightseeing

By India's standards, central Madras is a relatively young city, established as a fortified trading post by the East India Company in 1639. This was the Company's first foothold on the east coast of India.

Local cotton weavers and merchants were invited to settle around **Fort St George**, which thus formed the core of the new city. The principal export was cloth.

The textile industry is still dominant, and local companies produce clothing commissioned by some of the world's top fashion designers.

Fighting the French

The well-preserved fortress is enclosed with walls and ramparts, 20 feet thick. Within the fort, the principal buildings are used as government offices. Robert Clive came to work here in 1743 as an 18-year-old clerk. The Fort was captured by the French in 1746, but Clive escaped and soon began his meteoric military career. Madras returned to British hands two years later.

Clive became Governor of Madras at age 30. Behind St Mary's Church is the house where Clive lived and from which he was married in 1753. Madras remained as Britain's most important settlement until 1772 when the power centre shifted to Calcutta.

At Wellesley House close by, Sir Arthur Wellesley – the future Duke of Wellington – lived in 1798, during the period when he was posted to India.

Built with fortress-grade walls is **St Mary's Church** – India's oldest Anglican church, dating from 1680. Among those involved in financing the construction was a Boston-born official of the East India Company, Elihu Yale, who later became Governor. He then made a huge fortune, returned to America, and used some of his wealth to help found Yale University.

In the **Fort Museum** are many items relating to the early history of the East India Company.

Running south from Madras harbour is **Marina Beach**, which forms one of the world's longest sandy beaches. Between two and three hundred yards wide, it extends seven miles to the city boundaries, and then for many miles further.

Close to the beach is the **Parthasarathi Temple**, which was built probably in the 8th century AD by a Pallava king – member of a dynasty which ruled in South India from the 4th to the 9th centuries. Their cultural contribution was mainly architectural, with the temples at Mahabalipuram (see below) as their greatest monument.

Further along South Beach Road is the **Cathedral of San Thomé**, dedicated to St Thomas the Apostle ('Doubting Thomas') who is said to have preached on this spot. He was buried here after his martyrdom in 78 AD on St Thomas Mount near the present-day airport. The original Cathedral, rebuilt last century, was established by the Portuguese in 1504.

A mile inland from the Cathedral is the Shiva **Temple of Kapaleeswarar**, dominating the landscape with its enormous and colourful tower, 130 feet high. The best time to visit is at sunset, when ceremonies are held with musical accompaniment.

If time permits, the **National Art Gallery** and the **Government Museum** (for its fine collection of South Indian bronzes) are also worth visiting.

Shopping

As the chief market outlet for South India, the stores and hotel shopping arcades of Madras feature an immensely wide range of leather, silk and craft products.

The principal cottage-industry shops are located on Anna Salai Road which is still known by its former colonial name of Mount Road. The Victoria Technical Institute at 765 Mount Road offers the widest choice at reasonable prices with no need to haggle.

Some of the state emporia are rather a jumble, but the determined shopper can uncover dozens of low-cost handicrafts: sandalwood and rosewood products, children's toys, ceramics, miniature hanging lamps, textiles, leatherwork, papier-mâché items, batik paintings, silver and copper metalwork, votive images in bronze and stone.

Most of the cultured sales assistants can discourse on the traditions and locale of each craft, helping to build up each purchase into a complete 'conversation piece'.

7.2 Mahabalipuram

Parallel to the coast run the hills of the Eastern Ghats – an ancient rock formation, even older than the Himalayas. Thirty-seven miles south of Madras, an outcrop of granite at Mahabalipuram provided the work site for a great burst of rock-cut temple-building 1200 years ago.

For 60 years under the Pallava Kings, hundreds of sculptors worked the granite rocks into cave-temples, monolithic shrines, and the monumental two-spired **Shore Temple**. With shrines both for Vishnu and Shiva, it is the only survivor of a group of seven shore temples, the others having been washed away by the pounding waves.

The greatest display of unique sculpture is the **Descent of the Ganges**, claimed as the world's largest stone bas-relief, with carvings that form a complete pictorial record of Hindu mythology. Also known as **Arjuna's Penance**, the huge masterpiece measures 90 feet long by 30 feet high. Preserved from the 7th century AD, the sculptures depict life on the banks of the Holy Ganges: a lifesize elephant each side, gods, angels, holy men, and pilgrims bathing at the *ghats*. Over the centuries windborne sand and salt have worn smooth the finer details, but the overall impression is unforgettable.

Grouped around a life-size stone elephant are the Five *Rathas* – a word meaning temple chariots. They are monolithic shrines, carved into the form of miniature temples that are models of early Dravidian architecture.

During a brief stopover in Madras, Mahabalipuram comprises the outstanding tourist highlight of the South India circuit. En route, the road offers a panorama of rural India. There are plantations of tamarind trees (the fruit being an ingredient of curry), cashew nuts, eucalyptus and acacia.

Coconut groves give shade to little hamlets of fishermen, farmers or potters. In less fertile areas grow the sturdy palmyra palms, source of thatch, palm toddy and a bland fruit which is one of life's least memorable taste experiences.

7.3 Kanchipuram

Of lively human interest is the temple-town and pilgrimage centre of Kanchipuram, one of the seven sacred cities of Hindu India. Capital of the far-flung empire of the Pallava dynasty (4th to 9th centuries AD), the Golden City of a thousand temples is located 48 miles south-west of Madras. Kanchipuram rates a minimum five-hour excursion including sightseeing; or it can be combined on a full day's triangular circuit with Mahabalipuram.

These routes offer colourful views of rural India. Paddy fields are planted with high yield 'miracle' rice developed from the Philippines – two crops a year, or three if sufficient water resources are available.

Fields of jasmine, roses, chrysanthemums and lotus supply the flower markets of Madras. Vendors display heaped buds and blossoms in each little wayside village.

At Kanchipuram itself, non-Hindus are permitted entrance to the principal temples, except for the inner sanctums.

The largest temple, called **Ekambareswara**, was built between the 6th and 16th centuries during three successive dynasties. As the main Shiva temple, it features massive outer walls, gateway towers and a hall with a thousand pillars.

During festive seasons, the temple is alive with family groups of pilgrims, engrossed in their age-old rituals. A sacred mango tree, reputed to be 2500 years old, is the scene of fertility rites. Sterile women festoon the hanging branches with model cradles in the hope of being blessed with children.

Just outside town is the 8th century sandstone **Kailasanathar Temple**, built by the Pallava Kings. The outside structure is maintained by the Archaeological Department, while the inner sanctum is served by a hereditary family of priests.

Kanchipuram is a leading centre for handloom textiles. Sometimes a visit can be arranged to see cottage silk-weaving. The saris, dyed in attractive colours, are sold throughout India.

7.4 Madurai

Another famous temple town is Madurai, located on the banks of Vaigai river, 360 miles south of Madras. This second largest city in Tamil Nadu state was established over 2,500 years ago, and is a major centre of South Indian worship, art and culture. Here you can find ancient India in its purest and most exuberant form.

During the reign of the Tamil kings, around 2,000 years back, seats of academic Tamil learning flourished under generous royal patronage. Even today, Madurai is a prestigious regional centre of education.

The original lotus-shaped city has expanded with industrialisation, especially silk weaving and dyeing, but still preserves its ancient temples in a setting of paddy fields and coconut palms.

Madurai's greatest monument is the **Meenakshi Temple** which has nine massive towers, of which the tallest is 190 feet high. Each tower (called a *gopuram*) is totally covered in a riotous display of sculptures.

Here was the original focal point of the city, and the main temple gate is more like an entrance through a crowded and noisy bazaar. But all is peace and calm within the enormous temple complex and around the four-sided tank of the Golden Lily. Tradition says that this tank was used as a test of literary value. A manuscript would be placed on the water – sinking if worthless, floating if it had merit.

The Hall of a Thousand Pillars, built in mid-16th century, is richly decorated with lively sculptures, and doubles as a Tamil art gallery. Some pillars in the outer corridor are 'musical', producing a different note when tapped.

The **Tirumala Nayak Palace** was built in 1636 by one of the Nayak kings who ruled from AD 1559 until the dynasty's rule was ended by the British in 1781. The building in its Indo-Saracenic style was restored by order of the Governor of Madras in 1866, but is only a quarter of the original size.

The royal throne was sited in the octagonal Celestial Pavilion that faces the main entrance. The dome – 70 ft high and 60 ft across – is a remarkable architectural feat. By optical illusion, it seems to stand without any support.

7.5 Periyar Wild Life Sanctuary

The mountain ranges of South India offer the greatest possible contrast to the coastal fringes. The road from Madurai via the Periyar Wild Life Sanctuary to Cochin – a distance of 220 miles – crosses the Western Ghats.

It's a green landscape of lush forests, coconut gardens and tea and rubber plantations, liberally watered by the monsoons between May and November. There is the fragrance of spice in the air.

Midway between Madurai and Cochin, the Periyar Sanctuary is cradled in a valley centred on a vast lake formed by damming the Periyar river, some 3,000 feet above sea level.

A dense tropical jungle, 300 square miles in area, encircles the lake and up to the 6,000-ft level of the hills. This provides the natural habitat for elephant, antelope, leopard, wild boar, sambar (a species of deer), bison, sloth bear and an occasional tiger.

The best viewing season for a lake cruise is during the dry season of November to June, with February to June as the ideal. That's when forest water-holes dry up and the animals come more freely to the lake shores.

7.6 Cochin

The descent towards the coast passes through more plantations of cardamom and other spices, tea, coffee, rubber and pepper. At Kottayam there's the opportunity for a boat cruise along some of Kerala's backwaters. Here is another South Indian lifestyle. Every bend of the canal gives a different view of rural houses that nestle among the palms.

Spice trade

The port of Cochin, a cluster of peninsulas, townships and islands, has been the commercial outlet of Kerala since ancient times, thanks to one of the safest natural harbours on the southwest coast of India. Even 3,000 years ago, Phoenician traders came to deal in ivory, pearls and spices. Possibly from the 4th century AD, or maybe from the pre-Christian era, a Jewish colony was established and continued to flourish until most of the community moved to Israel in more recent years.

Otherwise, the first European colony in India was formed at Cochin by the Portuguese in 1500. Vasco da Gama established a trading station in 1502 and a fortress was built the following year. Cochin remained in Portuguese hands until the Dutch captured the city in 1663. Britain took over in 1795, and stayed until Indian independence in 1947.

Cochin's period of peak prosperity came during Dutch rule, when the spice trade was dominant. All the city's racial and religious groups shared in the prosperity.

Among the city's monuments are the **Synagogue** built in 1568, destroyed by the Portuguese in 1662 and rebuilt in 1664. Inscribed on a copper plate is the land grant given by a king of Cochin in the 7th century.

The **Dutch Palace** in Mattancherry was built by the Portuguese in 1555 and presented to the local Rajah. Coronation ceremonies of the Cochin rajahs were held in the central Coronation Hall of the palace. The building was modified by the Dutch, who then renamed it as the Dutch Palace. Large 17th-century murals depict scenes from the great Sanskrit epic poem called *Ramayana*. Others portray Shiva and Lord Krishna.

In Fort Cochin, **St Francis Church**, dating from 1510 is claimed to be the first church built by the Portuguese on Indian soil. Vasco da Gama died in Cochin in 1524 and was buried here until the remains were taken back to Portugal in 1538.

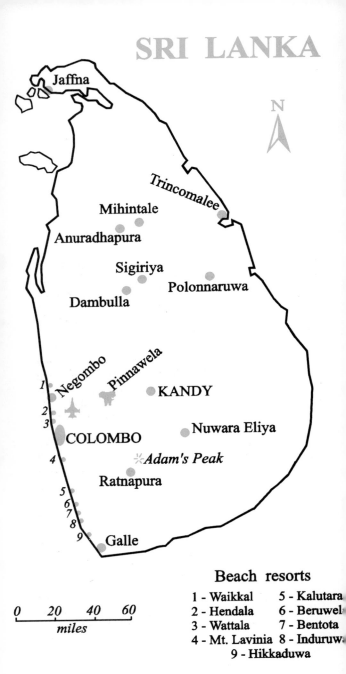

SRI LANKA

N

Jaffna

Trincomalee

Mihintale

Anuradhapura

Sigiriya

Polonnaruwa

Dambulla

Negombo   Pinnawela

1   KANDY

2

3

COLOMBO   Nuwara Eliya

4   ⁂*Adam's Peak*

Ratnapura

5

6

7

8

9   Galle

Beach resorts

1 - Waikkal   5 - Kalutara
2 - Hendala   6 - Beruwel
3 - Wattala   7 - Bentota
4 - Mt. Lavinia 8 - Induruw
9 - Hikkaduwa

0   20   40   60
miles

Chapter Eight

Sri Lanka

8.1 Enjoy your discoveries

Over the centuries, the island which hangs like a teardrop off the southern tip of India has had several changes of name. In 1972 Sri Lanka – meaning 'resplendent island' – reverted to its original name from 2,500 years ago, but was better known in more recent times as Ceylon.

Arab traders who came for spices and gem-stones called the island *Serendib*, which has contributed the word 'serendipity' to the English language – the faculty of making fortunate discoveries by accident. That derived from a Persian fairy-tale called *The Three Princes of Serendib*, in which the heroes possessed that gift.

Visitors have enjoyed making their happy discoveries around the island ever since.

Geographically, Sri Lanka is more than just a teardrop in the ocean. North to south is 270 miles, and 140 miles at the widest across. That's somewhat larger than Eire, with mountains three times higher, rainfall about the same as west-coast Ireland, but with temperatures that stay firmly in the mid-80s F. Sea-bathing temperatures are likewise in the blissful 80s.

The island's recorded history of 2,500 years is highlighted by the monuments of ancient cities which are listed as World Heritage sites. Major archaeological discoveries are still being made, thanks to a 'Cultural Triangle' project jointly conducted by UNESCO and the Sri Lankan Archaeological Department.

The earliest settlers in Sri Lanka brought in the rice-growing techniques of India. Early kings of the 5th century BC onwards gave the country great vitality and a well-ordered civilisation. Art and culture flourished with the advent of Buddhism as the island's main religion from 247 BC. Temples, monasteries, well-planned cities and palaces were built, while hydro engineers constructed a major system of irrigation reservoirs and canals. The basics of today's lifestyle come in direct line from 2,000 years ago – in its principal religion, festivals, music, dance, serenity and gift for contemplation.

The Portuguese arrived in 1505 to capture a monopoly of the spice trade. They introduced Christianity to the west-coast areas under their control. They were ousted in 1658 by the Dutch, who were also interested in spices and a different brand of Christianity. In turn came the British in 1796, who gained complete control of the island with the handover of Kandy in 1815.

Britain's discovery was the plantation system, worked by low-cost Tamil labour from South India. Coffee was planted in the hill country, to be replaced by the far more successful tea industry. Rubber plantations spread in the foothills, and coconut groves along the coastal fringe. All these cash crops, and the rice for home consumption, contribute to the lush green scenery.

Exotic flora and wildlife flourish in the plains and highlands, and beside rivers, lakes and waterfalls. Protected rain-forests and national parks give added sanctuary to birds, 242 species of butterflies, and animals such as leopard, monkeys, deer and around 4,000 to 4,500 wild elephants.

The world's first nature reserve was established at Mihintale near Anuradhapura in the 3rd century BC, to uphold the Buddhist principle of forbidding man to kill any form of life. Over 2000 years later, Mihintale still doubles as a wildlife sanctuary and a centre of pilgrimage.

The great 20th-century happy discovery is the beaches. Hundreds of miles of golden sand encircle the island, with off-shore islets, lagoons and coral gardens, coves and bays.

Uncrowded beaches

The coastal belt of palm trees ensures a green and shaded setting for the scattered plantations of holiday accommodation. All the watersport facilities are in place, with a total absence of crowds. From a beachside base you can enjoy making your own unexpected discoveries in this beautiful land. Note that some beaches are engulfed by the sea in monsoon time – May to October.

8.2 Arrival & orientation

On arrival at Katunayake Airport, Colombo, go through passport control with your completed immigration card. Next stop is currency control where your currency card is stamped and must be surrendered on departure.

It's worth bringing in your limit of 1½ litres of spirits for emergency use, such as full moon days when no liquor is served. After collecting your baggage and clearing customs, exit the hall. Baggage trolleys are free, but porters will want to help push your trolley for a tip. Give no more than 50 Rs, or maximum a £1 coin.

Outside, tour reps await their clients. The agency for Thomson Holidays is Aitken Spence Travels, who will arrange transfer to hotels.

The airport is located 20 miles north of Colombo on Sri Lanka's west coast. The nearest resort is at Negombo, north of the airport. Most other beach resorts are spread along the coast, up to 50 miles south of Colombo.

8.3 At your service

Money: The local currency is the Sri Lankan rupee, which is divided into 100 cents. Reckon between Rs.90 and Rs. 100 to the pound, or Rs.53 to Rs.60 to the US dollar, subject to fluctuation.

Exchange facilities are available at the airport, but you can easily change money at your hotel. But if you are going on tour, the airport gives the best rate. Banks are open Mon-Fri 9-13 hrs, and are closed weekends and all Bank Holidays including full moon days every month.

Well-known credit cards are widely accepted by shops, hotels and restaurants. Some shops try to add a percentage. This is not acceptable, and complaint should be made to the card company.

At the Hong Kong and Shanghai Bank, 24 Sir Baron Jayatillake Mawatha, Colombo 1, holders of Visa and Access/Mastercard can obtain cash advances or purchase travellers cheques.

Transport: Bus services are possibly the cheapest in Asia, but are tightly packed and not recommended. Trains are less crowded. Destination boards are in the national languages and in English.

Generally, Western visitors prefer to use taxis, which are readily available. Some are metered. Taxi drivers usually have enough English to get by. But make sure they clearly understand the destination required. Check that the 'flag' is turned down. On a longer journey, agree a price before setting off.

Driving in Sri Lanka demands a cool head, if only to avoid the suicidal cattle and dogs but also the eccentric habits of cyclists and pedestrians. Self drive is dangerous, but by western standards it costs relatively little extra to hire a driver with the car.

For sightseeing through the interior, it's far better to relax on an organised coach tour, with a knowledgeable and professional guide to explain all the diversity of sights and local customs. This is arranged by your rep.

8.4 Beaches of Sri Lanka

To many visitors, Sri Lanka is a land of eternal sunshine and wide golden beaches – ideal for relaxation, or for enjoying the variety of water sports. The waters of the Indian Ocean remain year-round at a minimum 75^0 F, clear and refreshing.

While Sri Lanka has over a thousand miles of palm-fringed beaches, holiday development has been concentrated down the south-western side of the island, mainly from Negombo (just north of Colombo airport) and south towards Galle.

There is an abundance of exotic underwater life worth seeing in those areas with off-shore coral reefs. But in some locations swimmers should take heed of local warnings of strong currents from May to October. Lagoons and rivers offer more potential for waterborne sports and excursions.

Negombo is typical of the relatively new beach-resort developments. Located 23 miles north of Colombo city, but only a 20-minute drive from the airport, Negombo has a long sandy beach, backed by a strip of rough road lined with gem and jewellery stores, bars, restaurants, boutiques and souvenir stands. Apart from the principal hotel, there's a modest range of accommodation from a couple of 3-star hotels to simple guest houses.

Negombo still keeps much of its original character as a fishing village, with lobster, crabs and prawns a speciality. There is fascination in seeing the traditional fishing craft such as outrigger canoes and catamarans that are still used to bring in fish such as seer, skipjack, herring and mullet.

The fish market is located at the southern end of Sea Street, close to the lagoon mouth where the Dutch built a fort to protect their trade in high-quality cinnamon. A surviving gateway is dated 1672. For transport, the Dutch did the obvious thing during their 130-year tenure and built a 75-mile network of canals. Britain's contribution to the local scene is a green used for weekend cricket, in a setting dominated by a spreading banyan tree.

The local community is mainly Roman Catholic, with an Easter Passion Play and enough churches to justify the town's description as a Little Rome.

About eight miles north of Negombo is **Waikkal**, set in a peaceful riverside location where the locals specialise in fishing and in tile-making. There is good potential for river trips and for bird-watching.

South of Negombo is **Hendala**, another traditional fishing village of palm-thatched houses.

Wattala is located closer to the northern outskirts of Colombo, with the busy port in the distance. The Dutch-built canal between Negombo and the capital can be explored along rough roads and rugged tracks. There are Catholic churches and Buddhist temples to visit.

South of Colombo, **Mt. Lavinia Beach** is the closest to the city centre, only 8 miles away. Its famous old-world hotel was once the residence of a colonial governor, Sir Thomas Maitland.

Further south is **Kalutara**, a resort with a varied history of trade and occupation by Arabs followed by Portuguese and Dutch in their quest for spices. Today its reputation comes especially from the mangosteen harvest. The fruit must ripen on the tree, and doesn't travel well. So seize your chance of sampling the juicy snow-white flesh of this orange-size fruit.

Kalutara is also the place to buy basket-ware, woven in colourful traditional designs of pink, black and red. The full range is displayed in the Basket Hall. Inland are rubber plantations. A Buddhist shrine called the Gangatillaka Vihara has a hollow interior with painted illustrations of Buddha's life.

Beruwela is a popular resort characterized by its typically Muslim architecture. Historically, Arab traders used to call here. Beruwela was probably one of the earliest Muslim settlements, dating from 1024 AD. The tomb of a Muslim saint is claimed to be a thousand years old.

Attracted by the excellent beach, a line of good hotels attracts numerous European visitors, with German as their principal language.

Separated from Beruwela by the Bentota River is the neighbouring resort of **Bentota**, located 36 miles south of Colombo, at the halfway stage to Galle. In a palm-tree setting with paddy fields in the distance, you can watch agile toddy tappers at work. They shin up coconut palms to collect liquid from pots that hang from every tree. The toddy can be drunk fresh, fermented or distilled.

Of sightseeing interest is the 13th-century temple called the Galapatha Vihara, which is treasured for its exquisite granite carvings from the early middle ages of Sri Lanka.

The Bentota River offers calm waters for windsurfing and sailing. It's possible to travel on a boat excursion further upstream to view the resident crocodiles.

Induruwa is a quiet resort with a beautiful beach, about three miles further south of Bentota. In this beach area is the Kosgoda Turtle hatchery, supervised by the Wild Life Protection Society of Sri Lanka.

Hikkaduwa is the most developed of Sri Lanka's beach resorts, enticing large numbers of younger-generation visitors by the water-sport potential, especially surfing, diving and exploration of underwater wrecks. The great attraction is a long stretch of spectacular coral reef, with all its rich and colourful variety of tropical fish and marine growth. You can even see turtle, peacefully swimming within the reef.

For those visitors who don't want to snorkel or scuba-dive, glass bottomed boats can offer breathtaking views of the underwater scene. The surfing area is south of the coral reef.

Hikkaduwa's four-kilometre strip is lined with lower-cost hotels, bars, restaurants and innumerable shops, and also doubles as the main coastal highway that continues south to Galle.

The seaport of **Galle**, in the southwest corner of the island is of great historic interest, with good sightseeing. From earliest times, Galle was a trading centre. Here the Portuguese established themselves in 1587 and built fortifications. The Dutch took over in 1640, strengthened the defensive system and gave the port its Dutch character which still survives.

Galle continued to function as Sri Lanka's principal seaport until the 1870s, when the artificial harbour at Colombo was built.

8.5 Colombo

As the country's administrative and commercial centre, Colombo is a lively city of 500,000 population, located 20 miles from Katunayake International Airport.

Colombo has been a trading centre for centuries, dealing in pearls, gem-stones and spices, though Galle in the southwest corner was initially more important. The more recent settlers – Portuguese, Dutch and British – have all left reminders of their period of occupation.

The focal point of Colombo is called Fort. Originally built by the Portuguese to protect the harbour, Fort housed Portuguese and Dutch garrisons during the 16th to 18th centuries. The original walls have disappeared and only a couple of cannon remain.

Colombo's main expansion dates from the 19th century, when Britain converted the port into one of the world's largest artificial harbours. Today, Fort is the prosperous commercial heart of the city, where visitors can buy gems, brass and silverware.

Among the principal landmarks is the Lighthouse Clock Tower, built in 1837. In a spacious location opposite the gleaming white General Post Office is the former home of the colonial governors, now used as the President's House. Old Parliament Building, facing the Indian Ocean, houses the Presidential Secretariat.

A new Parliament complex of classical oriental design is located seven miles away at Sri Jayawardanapkura Kotte, the country's administrative capital.

Pettah

Adjoining Fort is Pettah, the city's teeming bazaar area which also includes numerous mosques, temples and Colombo's oldest Dutch church. Here is all the colour and chaos of the Orient. The Dutch Period Museum, at 95 Prince Street in the bazaar area, is a restored building – originally the Dutch town hall – with a peaceful courtyard.

Train buffs could visit the Fort Railway Station for its collection of antique railway equipment.

Just south of Fort is Galle Face Green, a grassy promenade spread along a mile of seafront. It is specially lively at weekends.

Upmarket Colombo

Three miles south of Fort is the fashionable area of Cinnamon Gardens – Colombo 7 – with spacious mansions and embassies. In this wealthy district is Vihara Maha Devi Park, more briefly known until the 1950s as Victoria Park.

Flowering trees are ablaze with colour from March till early May. Close by, the National Museum – founded in 1877 – houses a wide collection of ancient sculpture and other relics.

Still further south is Dehiwala Zoo, where elephants have been trained to dance every afternoon at 17.15 hrs. Spread over a large area, the Zoo is well laid out and is rated among the best in Asia. Open 8-18 hrs daily.

8.6 Shopping

Shops are open Mon-Fri 9-17 hrs, and many are also open Saturdays until 1 pm. Best buys are handicrafts, produced by labour-intensive methods to high standards of design and workmanship.

Shopping for quality handicrafts can be done under one roof in stores operated by the Sri Lanka Handicrafts Board. These stores are located on York Street and at Liberty Plaza in Colombo, and in several tourist resorts and provincial centres.

The choice is bewildering: sterling and plated silverware, every imaginable object made of brass, lacquer ware, pottery and papier-mâché. There are highly decorative demon masks, wood-carvings, batik fabrics, handloom textiles, terracotta pottery, drums and flutes. Exquisite lace is produced by methods taught by the Portuguese in the 16th century.

Precious and semi-precious gems are Sri Lanka's most famous export: blue, yellow, pink, orange, white and star sapphires, rubies, cat's eyes, alexandrite, quartz, moonstones, zircons, garnets, amethysts and topaz.

The State Gem Corporation (Macan Markar Building, 24 York Street, Colombo) or the Ratnapura Gem Bureau guarantee the stones they sell, and are the most reliable outlets for the higher-priced stones. But hundreds of dealers can offer more moderately priced jewellery set with semi-precious gem-stones.

Unless you really know the business, don't listen to any sales pitch about buying stones in quantity for reselling at huge profit outside Sri Lanka.

Tea export is restricted to three kilos, any excess being subject to an export duty. The Tea Centre, operated by the Tea Promotion Board in Colombo at 574 Galle Road, sells special gift packages of selected brands.

All the spices mentioned in the next section are readily available, especially in Kandy and at the Peradeniya Botanic Gardens. Many private spice gardens are open to the public and sell direct.

8.7 Eating out, and Nightlife

Resort hotels offer a full range of international cuisine. You will also find European, Chinese, Indian and Japanese restaurants.

Sri Lankan cookery is spicy and exciting. Rice and red-hot curry is standard fare. Curries can include a complete alphabetical listing of spices: cardamon, chilli, cinnamon, clove, coriander, cummin, fenugreek, garlic, green ginger, mustard and pepper. Hotels soften the impact by toning down the chilli or increasing the base of coconut milk. If your mouth catches fire, douse the heat with buffalo-milk curds or chew some fresh coconut.

Seafood is particularly good. Lobster is expensive, but there is excellent choice of crab, prawn and squid, grouper, fresh tuna or trout. Meat dishes including buffalo are inexpensive, and are usually curried. Steaks are not recommended as local beef is usually tough.

Something different are pan hoppers – small rice pancakes that make a base for varied dishes from scoops of curry to honey and yoghourt. Fried egg hoppers are specially popular for breakfast; or you could spread plain hoppers with marmalade and butter, hoping the locals won't notice.

Sri Lanka is rich in its year-round variety of fruit and vegetables, thanks to tropical conditions in the lowlands and a temperate climate in the highlands. Papaya, pineapple, banana and mango are always available, with refreshment from king coconut juice. Other fruits such as mangosteen, avocado pear, durian, rambuttan, passion fruit, oranges and grape-fuit are harvested mainly between July and August.

A number of rice-flour desserts are sweetened with palm treacle, which tastes something like maple syrup.

Thirst-quenchers: Don't drink tap water. Bottled water is safer. Most hotels fill bedroom flasks with filtered water which should cause no upsets. Imported canned drinks are available, but expensive. Of course Coca-Cola is there, and a local imitation called Elephant House – a brand-name which appears on other soft drinks. There's also lemonade and ginger beer.

The country's own home brew is arrack, a high-octane distilled coconut toddy which can readily be mixed with soft drinks. Beer is also locally produced – a Pilsner type, low in alcohol. But you can also buy imported lagers. A hotel beer will cost roughly Rs.50, or gin and tonic Rs.30. Away from your hotel, avoid ice in your drinks.

Tea, of course, is everywhere, usually served very strong. Sample the different types, to decide which brands you wish to take home.

Nightlife

The big hotels feature dinner dancing, an occasional floor show, and sometimes a cultural performance of Kandyan dances or devil dancing. Check with newspapers or hotel desks for details. Colombo has some steamy night clubs. If these alternatives do not appeal, pack some good books.

8.8 Quick facts

Total area: 25,630 sq miles – the size of Southern Ireland, or half the size of New York State.
Coastline: 837 miles.
Time: GMT plus 5½ hrs.
Natural resources: limestone, phosphates, gemstones.
Land use: arable land 16%; permanent crops 17%; meadows and pastures 7%; forest and woodland 37%; other 23%.
Population: 18,000,000, growth rate 1.2%
Life expectancy: 69 years male, 74 years female.
Fertility rate: 2.3 children born per woman.
Ethnic groups: Sinhalese 74%, Tamil 18%.
Languages: Sinhala, Tamil and English.
Religion: Buddhist 69%, Hindu 15%, Christian 8%, Muslim 8%.
Work force: 6,600,000; farming 46%, mining and industry 13%, commerce and transport 12%, services etc 28%.
Literacy: male 91%, female 81%.
Capital: Colombo, population 660,000.
Independence: 4 February 1948 (from UK).
Government: a democratic socialist republic.
Legal system: a blend of English common law, Roman-Dutch, Muslim and customary law.
Executive branch: president, prime minister, cabinet.
Judicial branch: Supreme Court.
Political parties: United National Party (UNP), Sri Lanka Freedom Party (SLFP) and others with smaller support.
Suffrage: universal at age 18.

The economy: inflation and unemployment are high, but economic conditions are improving. Plantation crops, gemstones and textiles are the main currency earners. Tourism comes about fourth down the list.

Farming: occupies almost half the workforce, with tea, rubber and coconuts yielding 35% of export earnings. Other crops include rice, sugarcane, pulses and spices.

8.9 Festivals and public holidays

A great delight for visitors to Sri Lanka is the number of public holidays and festivals – around 30 days a year – though it can be most frustrating for a business traveller. Quite apart from the weekend breaks, there are some secular or political holidays:

Jan 14 – Tamil Tahi Pongal harvest festival day
Feb 4 – Independence Day
April – Two days' Sinhala and Tamil New Year
May 1 – May Day
May 22 – National Heroes' Day
Dec 31 – Special Bank Holiday

In addition, all the principal Buddhist, Hindu, Christian and Moslem religious holidays are kept as public holidays, including Easter, Christmas, the end of Ramadan and Mohammed's birthday.

Besides all these, every full moon day is a holiday, called *poya*, when all places of entertainment are closed and no liquor is sold. Hotels arrange for guests to give their drink orders on the previous day.

If Monday or Friday are poya days, many local people take off on long weekend trips, crowding the transport and accommodation facilities.

Virtually every month sees at least one or two highly colourful Buddhist or Hindu festivals, which are fascinating for visitors. Because of dependence on the moon, dates shift from year to year. Check the calendar when you arrive!

8.10 Hints and useful addresses

Security: There is long-standing conflict between the Sri Lankan government and a Tamil separatist group, the Liberation Tigers of Tamil Eelam (LTTE). Military actions may continue in northern and eastern areas of the island, where travel restrictions are enforced. These locations are far removed from the international resort areas. Just take care to follow any local advice.

Electricity: 230/240 volts AC, 50 Hz. Round 3-pin plugs are usual, with bayonet lamp fittings.

Telephone: To avoid the usual hotel mark-ups on international phone calls, buy a Payphone Card which can be used from public phones.

From abroad, the dialling for Sri Lanka is +94 followed by area code and the local number.

Dress: When entering a temple or monument, visitors should remove shoes. Take a pair of socks, as the ground can burn the soles of your feet. You are not allowed to visit some temples in shorts.

Elsewhere, informality is the rule, but swimwear should be worn only by the pool or on the beach. Topless and nude bathing is banned! Lightweight cotton clothing is ideal, but pack a sweater and medium weight slacks for hill country. An umbrella is useful, if only for sightseeing in the open sun.

Tipping: A service charge is generally included in your bill, and tipping is optional. Carry some small change if you want to tip guides when sightseeing.

Departure: Individual travellers must pay a departure tax of Rs.500, which is settled direct by some tour operators such as Thomson Holidays. Change any left-over local currency. The first-floor duty-free shop, cafe and bar use foreign currency only.

Photography: Visitors are welcome to photograph Buddha statues and other religious images. But do not drape yourself alongside them, nor expect the saffron robed Buddhist monks to pose for a picture.

Useful addresses:
Sri Lankan Tourist Board (UK), 13 Hyde Park Gardens, London W2 2LU.
Tel: (0171) 262 5009 or 262 1841. Fax: 262 7970.
Open Mon-Fri 9-17 hrs.

High Commission for the Republic of Sri Lanka, 13 Hyde Park Gardens, London W2 2LU.
Tel: (0171) 262 1841.

Sri Lankan Embassy, 2148 Wyoming Avenue, N.W., Washington, D.C. 20008. Tel: (202) 4834 025/8. There are consulates in New York, Los Angeles, New Orleans and Newark.

Addresses in Colombo
Tourist Information Centre, 321 Galle Road, Colombo 3. Tel: 573175.
Gives advice on Sri Lankan culture, customs, history, etc. Open Mon-Fri 08.00-16.45 hrs; weekends and public holidays until 12.30 hrs.
Ceylon Tourist Board, P.O. Box 1504, 78 Steuart Place, Colombo 3. Tel: (1) 437 059. Fax: 437 953.

Aitken Spence Tours (representing Thomson Holidays), Lloyds Buildings, Sir Baron Mawatha, P.O. Box 5, Colombo. Tel: 430892. Fax: 436382.

British Embassy, 190 Galle Road, P.O. Box 1433, Colombo 3. Tel: 437336.

U.S. Embassy, 210 Galle Rd., P.O. Box 106, Colombo. Tel: 448007.

Chapter Nine
Exploring Sri Lanka

9.1 Away from the beaches

Few countries are free of security problems. Since 1983 Sri Lanka has occasionally burst into the headlines, with violence from Tamil separatists. At risk is the north-east corner of the island, and some parts of the east coast. There have also been incidents in Colombo itself – which explains heavy army and police presence throughout the city.

There seems virtually nil risk to visiting holidaymakers, as at the time of writing we hear of no tourist having been harmed throughout the long period of the troubles. But it's sensible to avoid problems, by heeding local warnings to stay well clear of the Jaffna peninsula and similar unsettled areas. It's inadvisable to hire a self-drive car with the intention of exploring the off-limits region.

Fortunately the great sightseeing highlights of Sri Lanka are in trouble-free areas. On sightseeing tours, operators will aim to ensure that you go nowhere near any zone which may be under threat.

From the beach resorts of the southwest coast, the principal sites can be covered in a one-week circuit, to include the 'Cultural Triangle' of Kandy, Anuradhapura (around 130 miles from Colombo), Polonnaruwa and World Heritage Sites such as the Dambulla Rock Temple and the 5th century AD Sigiriya Rock Fortress.

Otherwise, from the beach resorts of the southwest coast, a number of whole-day excursions are available, or longer trips which include overnight accommodation. They offer a good selection of the places visited on a more comprehensive tour. Ask your tour rep for details of the various itineraries.

Much interest comes from all the tiny details seen when driving through the tropical countryside: buffaloes grazing in the shade of a tree; the shades of green of individual rice paddies; the motionless white egrets that look like decorative statues.

Then there are hundreds of human details that reflect the local lifestyle: rubber-tappers at work; women pounding clothes in a rippling stream; children in white uniforms, returning from school; Buddhist monks in saffron-coloured robes, seeking alms in a market town.

With a well-trained guide, a myriad customs can be explained, bringing more understanding to what you see. It becomes a memorable part of the holiday experience.

Here's a short list of places worth including in your sightseeing plans.

9.2 Ratnapura

High into the hill country, with magnificent scenery and views of 7300-ft Adam's Peak, Ratnapura lies about 40 miles inland from the coast. Virtually every village en route has its specialized industry. A typical community produces rattan furniture; then comes a village with wayside stalls that are stacked with packaged cashew nuts. A neighbouring settlement makes flower pots, while a mile or two further you're into pineapple country. Finally, past paddy fields and towards the tea-planting areas, you'll see numerous gem-mining pits.

Ratnapura (meaning 'Gem City') is Sri Lanka's principal centre for the mining, cutting and polishing industries.

Sri Lanka has been world famous for its multicoloured gem stones for over 2,000 years, with the range of sapphires as the greatest of the island's gem-stone assets. Once a mine site has been decided upon, the blessings of the gods are sought, with ritual ceremonies and prayers for success of the venture.

Behind the glittering stones in shop displays is a long tradition in gem cutting and polishing to bring out their glow and sparkle. For a more complete understanding of the local industry, it's worth visiting Ratnapura's Gem Museum, which displays a prized collection of blue sapphires, rubies, cat's eyes, amethysts, alexandrites, garnets, zircons and moonstones.

Adam's Peak, which dominates the skyline, is a pilgrimage site thanks to the huge 'sacred footprint' of Adam (or possibly Buddha or Lord Shiva). From Ratnapura, energetic devotees make a 7-hour climb by lamp-light to the mountain top, normally during the pilgrimage season of December to April. The aim is to watch the sunrise. Easier climbs start from the other side of the mountain.

A visit to Ratnapura makes an excellent one-day trip from the coastal resorts. But longer tours continue to Nuwara Eliya and Kandy, past the prime tea gardens of the hill country.

Tea came to the economic rescue from 1867, after the former plantation crop of coffee was killed off by blight. Facing ruin, the estate owners switched to the cultivation of tea, newly introduced by a Scottish planter who had made trial plantings of seedlings from China and from Assam in India.

Since then, tea production has become one of the island's most important industries. Sri Lanka has now become the world's leading tea exporter, overtaking India. The island accounts for more than a quarter of the world's international tea trade.

Plantation visits can show the field work of hand plucking, followed by the factory processes of withering, rolling, fermenting, drying and grading. Tea grows up terraced mountain slopes almost to the 8,000 feet level. Quality is best above Kandy.

9.3 Nuwara Eliya

In the beautiful heart of tea-growing country, Nuwara Eliya is a British-built hill station that would make Queen Victoria feel at home. Six thousand feet up, this summer retreat is fossilized in the old world charm of colonial days. Nineteenth-century tea planters' houses are modelled like those in a prosperous English village.

The resort offers well-stocked trout streams, seasonal horse-racing, good walking potential and one of Asia's best golf courses. Visitors should come prepared for rain and chilly evenings. The dramatic World's End viewpoint commands a sheer 3,500-ft drop to the valley below.

9.4 *Kandy*

More tea plantations can be seen en route to Kandy, the former royal capital which fell to British troops in 1815. This ancient stronghold of the Sinhala kings is specially rich in cultural history. Dating from the centuries of royal patronage, the arts and crafts, music and dance still flourish.

The lakeside Temple of the Tooth (Dalada Maligawa) is dedicated to a Sacred Tooth of Buddha and is a holy shrine for all Sri Lankan Buddhists. Daily rituals with drums and flutes pay homage to the relic.

A major festival – Procession of the Sacred Tooth – is held annually in July-August, with hundreds of dancers, drummers and at least seventy well-dressed and decorated elephants in the torch-lit parades. For ten successive nights the 3-mile procession is repeated, each time with still more elephants until the final climax on the night of the full moon.

If you happen to be in Sri Lanka during this Sacred Tooth Festival, make every possible effort to attend! It would cost Hollywood millions of dollars to mount an equivalent production. In Sri Lanka, every volunteer performer belongs to one of the numerous village groups who are proud to participate.

In the balmy night air, the full moon presides over the procession that starts with the cracking of whips like pistol shots. Blazing torches are fuelled by burning copra. Frenzied dancers spin their torches like catherine wheels to the thunder of drums, the wailing of oboes and the blowing of conches that sound like fog-horns. There are jugglers, flag-wavers, acrobats and stilt-walkers. Child groups dance around maypoles that are carried and steadied by a team of adults.

But the great stars are the elephants, festooned with battery-powered fairy lights on their trunk, tusks and ears. The animals seem to enjoy the procession, showing their pleasure by swaying their trunks and twitching their illuminated ears.

Next to the enormous Temple of the Tooth is the National Museum, in a building where the royal concubines were housed.

Behind the Temple is an Archaeological Museum which occupies other remnants of the royal palace.

Numerous other major temples, monasteries and meditation centres are located in and around Sri Lanka's second-largest city.

Of special interest are the Royal Botanical Gardens at **Peradeniya**, just outside Kandy in a riverside setting. Their origins date from the 14th century, but the 150-acre site was laid out in 1821 as the Kandyan queen's Pleasure Garden. During British occupation, the garden was converted to scientific botanical use. Today, some four thousand plant species are cultivated, including virtually every variety of spice from cinnamon, nutmeg and cloves to cardamom and pepper.

In this botanist's paradise is the giant bamboo of Burma – the largest known bamboo, with 10-inch diameter stems that grow 12 inches per day. The bamboo comes useful in house-building, as water spouts etc; or as umbrella stands.

In contrast to magnificent avenues of Palm trees, the orchid collection features striking displays of rare tropical and semi-tropical hybrids that are being bred for commercial use.

9.5 Elephant Orphanage

From Kandy, some tours return to their coastal base with a pause to visit the Elephant Orphanage at **Pinnawela**, near Kegalle. Established in 1975, the

Orphanage ranks as Sri Lanka's most popular elephant attraction, especially when it's mealtime in the nursery or bathtime in the river.

The elephant problem is that Sri Lanka's human population has risen during the present century from three to eighteen million. Large areas of the elephants' jungle habitat have been cleared for human settlement.

Today the wild elephant population is estimated at between 4,000 to 4,500 - compared with almost 20,000 at the beginning of the 19th century. Even though national parks and other protected areas have been set aside, it's difficult for the animals to re-adjust their home ranges to fit in with human requirements. Captive breeding can help keep the species alive, by reintroducing it to its wild habitat.

Incidentally, poaching is not a problem, as only a percentage of Asian male elephants have tusks.

9.6 Mihintale and Anuradhapura

Longer tours of Sri Lanka continue north to a trio of ancient cities: Sigiriya, Polonnaruwa and Anuradhapura. A few miles east of Anuradhapura is **Mihintale**, where Buddhism was introduced to Sri Lanka in 247 BC through conversion of the reigning king. A group of missionaries from northern India then settled here in hermit caves. From this base, the new religion swept through the land, where it is still the predominant faith.

Many hundreds of granite steps (1,840 to be precise) await pilgrims and tourists, whose efforts are rewarded by spectacular views.

En route to the summit are varied monastic remains – shrines, a refectory and two pagodas (which locally are called dagobas).

As the island's capital from 4th century BC to 10th century AD, and its most ancient religious centre, **Anuradhapura** still ranks as a place of pilgrimage.

The most remarkable relic is the Sacred Bo Tree, decorated with gifts and frangipani. Completely authentic, it dates from the 3rd century BC, grown

from a sapling of the original Bo Tree in northern
India where Buddha found enlightenment.

The city was a model of civic planning, with
separate areas for different social classes. Engineers
built large reservoirs or 'tanks' to ensure a depend-
able water supply for domestic use and irrigation.
Anuradhapura was finally abandoned as the capital,
due to successive invasions from south India.

Major research and renovation of the surviving
monuments is being continued by the Archaeological Department in cooperation with UNESCO.

9.7 Dambulla

A popular base for exploring the Cultural Triangle
sites is the Kandalama Hotel at Dambulla, built
down the dramatic cliff face of a granite outcrop.
On the edge of a virgin jungle, teeming with birdlife, the hotel overlooks the very large man-made
lake reservoir called Kandalame Wewa.

In the Dambulla area is a vast granite rock mass,
a mile round the base and 500 feet high. During the
1st century BC, rock caves sheltered the exiled
King Valagam Bahu for 14 years, while his throne
was occupied by Tamil invaders.

When the king regained power, he launched a
magnificent cave-temple project, to include a 50-ft
reclining Buddha in the first cave. The wall and
ceiling frescoes were added during the 15th to 18th
centuries.

Even more magnificent, the second cave contains
around 150 statues of Hindu deities, with still more
frescoes that depict scenes from the life of Buddha,
and the great episodes of Sri Lankan history.

9.8 Sigiriya

About 12 miles from Dambulla is the Sigiriya Rock
Fortress, one of Sri Lanka's most spectacular
sights, built over 1500 years ago. Shaped like the
core of an ancient volcano, the rock was converted
during the 5th century AD into a fortress with a

four-acre 128-room palace on top. It is visible from the Dambulla site.

The builder, named Kasyapa, was involved in a bitter family feud – firstly with his father, the king, whom he imprisoned and murdered; then with his half-brother who was heir to the throne. The building of the royal palace in the sky continued for 18 years, and finally ended when Kasyapa committed suicide to avoid his brother's vengeance.

In later centuries the site was used as a monastery, but then fell into disuse.

The outer defences were well planned, with a surrounding moat that was equipped with very sharp stakes planted below water level, and stocked with crocodiles. To reach the summit, 600 feet above, was a question of clambering up some 1,200 steps, easily defended.

Today's visitors come first to a water garden – one of the world's oldest surviving water features. During the monsoon season, some of the fountains are active. At a higher level is a terrace garden.

Most visitors continue climbing still higher, to reach the voluptuous frescoes of bare-breasted women, who are endlessly reproduced in tourist literature. Originally, the outer surface of the rock was decorated with over 500 frescoes of 'cloud maidens' who may have been goddesses or more likely were dancing girls.

Owing to action of the elements, only 19 frescoes remain. Until recent years there were more, but they were vandalised with tar. The young ladies are now protected by strict security.

At a higher level is the 'mirror wall', with a highly polished surface on which visitors of long-past centuries have recorded their impressions. A dedicated academic has published a complete translation of the graffiti.

Beyond is the last stage - the lion's paw entrance. Today the brick and stucco lion is not there, having broken and eroded away. But his paw remains, still guarding the final access to the ruined palace above. However, many people cannot make the full distance. Out of breath, they return to base after seeing the frescoes.

9.9 Polonnaruwa

The remarkable ruined city of Polonnaruwa was capital of the medieval kings who rose to power after the decline of Anuradhapura. The city reached its dazzling peak in the 12th century. The royal citadel was enclosed by walls 21 miles long by 12 miles wide – about the area of present-day London!

To keep the population in water and rice, the kings built an enormous irrigation tank, occupying over nine square miles and known as the Sea of Parakrama. The royal philosophy was "let not a drop of water reach the sea, without having served man before reaching the sea." Thanks to the irrigation system, the surrounding plain became one of the great rice granaries of the East.

After devastating invasions in later centuries, the irrigation tank reverted to jungle, until British engineers restored the entire system, which still operates. Visiting children and adults enjoy a swim or take a bath in this huge lake which has been stocked with Japanese carp.

The main sights of Polonnaruwa today are the sacred temples and the royal palace of King Parakrama Bahu the Great who ruled for 33 years; the carved rock statue of the King; and the giant stone Buddha carvings of Gal Vihara.

The 12th-century palace of King Parakrama stood seven storeys high. Later, all the wooden parts of the palace were burnt, so that the upper floors collapsed. But the massive foundation walls survived, to give some idea of the magnificence of the original building. Close by is the handsome Royal Bath, the Kumara Poluna. The beautiful Council Hall is remarkably well preserved, with elephant carvings around the base and a dragon balustrade at the entrance.

The frequency of elephant images is a reminder of their importance in ancient times. They were used for work purposes, for religious festivals, for pageants and even as battle tanks. In addition, elephants were a very conspicuous way of displaying a person's wealth.

Power building

The king could demonstrate his power and wealth by the number of his concubines, but he also did much for Buddhism and for agriculture. A later king went virtually bankrupt in his efforts to maintain the building momentum, and then new invasions from India led to relocation of the capital.

The entire cluster of monuments was abandoned and overgrown, until archaeologists embarked on the long program of exploration and renewal which now has the continued support of UNESCO.

Much of the sprawling site is covered with the remains of religious buildings. Although the remains are not in active religious use, visitors are requested to remove their shoes and hats before entering each sanctuary. The diversity of architectural styles is remarkable.

The **Image House** – Thuparama – is an oblong brick building with a vaulted roof. The shrine contains an image of the Buddha. Close by is a red-brick circular relic house called the **Vatadage**, built in the 12th century.

The pillars supported a wooden roof and at all four cardinal points there are statues of the Buddha. Well-preserved guard-stones, moonstones and sculptured texts embellish the monument.

In total contrast is the **Satmahal Prasada**, a square 7-storey pyramid-shaped tower, built during the 12th century when travelling monks returned with architectural ideas from Cambodia.

Gal Vihare is a group of the most impressive stone carvings in Sri Lanka. Four huge statues of the Buddha are carved from an outcrop of granite rock. There is Buddha in meditation in the lotus posture; inside the cave is another Buddha, also in the lotus posture. The third statue is a standing Buddha, with arms folded, in a state of serenity; and finally a Buddha reclining, asleep.

In between the standing statue and the cave entrance are some inscriptions which lay down the code of conduct for monks: the time for getting up in the morning; the time for meals; how monks should comport themselves in public and how they should conduct their spiritual activities.

Chapter Ten

The Maldive Islands

10.1 Watersport paradise

The Maldives comprise 1,200 tiny coral islands that stretch southwest of Sri Lanka for 500 miles in a chain of 26 atolls. Their total land area is a mere 115 square miles – less than the Isle of Wight, or 1½ times Washington DC. The locals inhabit 200 of the islands, leaving the rest to anyone who wants to play Robinson Crusoe, eating fish and coconuts.

Historians say the Maldives were settled by Sri Lankans in 5th century AD. Arab traders introduced Islam in the 12th century. British protection came in 1887, followed by Independence in 1965.

By air, several connections weekly are by a 90-minute 484-mile flight from Colombo to Malé, the Maldivian capital. A two-centre holiday can combine Sri Lankan beaches or sightseeing with a week or two of coral island relaxation or water sport.

Inter-island transport is aboard a local boat called *dhoni*. At Malé airport, these craft wait like taxis to transport passengers to their chosen resorts. Faster travel is also possible by speedboats which take 45 minutes to Rannalhi, 20 minutes to Lohifushi, and 15 minutes to Taj Lagoon.

One-fourth of the population earns a living from fishing, and the government gets licence fees from foreign fleets that catch tuna and bonito in the great expanse of territorial waters. But the principal economic growth now comes from tourism.

Resorts are based on beaches and water sports. Sea temperatures range 80-86° F year-round, and often reach almost blood heat in the lagoons.

Hills are rarely more than nine feet above sea level. All tourist accommodation is sited on formerly uninhabited islands, to avoid upsetting Islamic culture. Nude or topless bathing is illegal, modest dress is expected outside of the resorts, and personal import of duty-free liquor is forbidden. However, on these holiday islands, alcohol is available but served by non-Muslim Sri Lankan bartenders.

There is only one hotel development per island. A half-hour beach stroll takes you right around your coral paradise. Other possible activities are idyllic windsurfing, water-skiing and snorkelling.

The blue lagoons are like tropical aquariums. Swimmers share the water with teeming marine life, from Napoleon wrasse to parrotfish. Shoals glide like a well-trained ballet along the walls of coral.

Game fishermen sail out for grouper, blue marlin and shark. For anyone who prefers just looking, dolphins play, and flying fish leap from the waves.

Otherwise the big sport is scuba diving, with great variety of coral sites. Conditions are perfect for novices and qualified divers alike. If you want to learn, each resort has a diving school.

10.2 Quick facts

Coastline: 520 miles.
Time: GMT plus 5 hrs.
Natural resources: fish.
Land use: arable land 10%; meadows and pastures 3%; forest and woodland 3%; other 84%.
Population: 270,000, growth rate 3.5%
Life expectancy: 65 years male, 68 years female.
Fertility rate: 6 children born per woman.
Ethnic groups: Sinhalese, Dravidian, Arab and African.
Languages: Divehi, a Sinhala dialect; and English.
Religion: Sunni Muslim.
Work force: 66,000; 25% engaged in fishing.
Literacy: male 93%, female 93%.
Capital: Malé.
Independence: 26 July 1965 (from UK).
Government: a republic.
Political parties: no organised political parties.

Suffrage: universal at age 21.
Executive branch: president, cabinet.
Legal system: based on Islamic law, with some English common law in commercial subjects.
Judicial branch: High Court.

The economy: based on fishing, tourism and shipping, with tourism now accounting for 60% of foreign exchange earnings. Fishing is now second in economic importance. Industry is limited mainly to clothing production, boat building and handicrafts.

10.3 At your service

Entry: A 30-day visa is given free on arrival.
Money: About 18 Maldivian Rufiya (Rf) to the pound, or Rf 11 to the US $. One Rf = 100 Laari. US dollars are standard currency in resorts, but sterling and other Western banknotes, traveller cheques and major credit cards are acceptable.
Banks are open 9-13 hrs, Sun-Thu; offices 7.30-13.30, Sat-Thu; shops 8-23 daily, Fri 14.30-23 hrs.
Tipping is officially discouraged, but it's normal to reward good service.
Language: The Maldivians speak Divehi, a dialect of Singhalese, with writing based on Arabic.
Holidays: In this Muslim country, Friday is the day of rest. There are seven national holidays: Jan 1; Jan 13 Martyr's Day; Mar 20 Hajj Day; July 26 Independence Day; Aug 9-10 National Day; Nov 3 Victory Day; Nov 11 Republic Day. Some of these dates are approximate, varying with the moon.

Five more holidays have floating dates, based on Islamic festivals from Ramadan onwards.